Present and Powerful

A Journey to Resilience, Emotional Intelligence, and Bold Leadership

Copyright

Present and Powerful: A Journey to Resilience, Emotional Intelligence, and Bold Leadership

©2025 Copyright by Donna Davis

All Rights Reserved.

No part of this book may be reproduced, stored in a retrieval system, or transmitted by any means without the written permission of the author.

Printed in the United States of America.

ISBN: 978-1-7377868-3-2

Imprint: D W Davis Consulting, LLC

Books may be purchased in bulk quantity and/or special sales by contacting the author at dwdavisconsulting@gmail.com

Book Cover Designed and Publishing Assistance by Reaching While Teaching LLC
www.reachingwhileteaching.com

Foreword

I have known Donna for more than 10 years, and although I've seen her perseverance over the years when faced with difficult situations, reading this book gave me a deeper appreciation for the person she is. The chapters of her life have shaped a woman of conviction who holds fast to her ethics and integrity, and a faith in God that is indisputable.

In a world where many are searching for their true purpose and questioning themselves, 'Why am I here?', this book will inspire and encourage you to face your truth, your story, and to honestly come to the realization that you matter. This will be a time of forgiveness, healing, and living your best life, as God has ordained it just for you.

You will find that Donna is honest and reveals everything. The pretty and the not-so-pretty. She is truly authentic in what she has experienced and how it has shaped her into the person she is today. I recommend this book to you as a true-life journey of a woman who at one time thought "she would never be enough…and the woman who now knows she always was."

It is my honor to write this foreword, and I believe you will indeed find something in this book that will enrich your journey. Extend grace to yourself and walk in your God ordained calling.

Diane D. Gillie
A Friend, Columbia, SC

Prologue

I remember only having enough money for a single candy bar.

I remember its flavor, Snickers. Chocolate, peanuts, and soft nougat. The kind of sweetness that didn't just satisfy my taste buds but wrapped itself around my tired soul. I hadn't started with that one; I'd tried a few others first. But over time, Snickers became my choice, a small, edible promise of what I believed was yet to come.

The convenience store wasn't anything special, just a modest shop along my walk home, one I'd passed countless times without stepping inside. After long days of pushing through exhaustion, I'd stop in, carrying hope like a carefully rationed budget line item. I would count my coins twice before placing them on the counter.

That candy bar wasn't an indulgence; it was a quiet declaration of my worth, even in moments when I felt undeserving. Among the noise of my own negative self-talk, it reminded me that I still mattered.

It wasn't about sugar. It was about sanity.
It wasn't about candy. It was about faith.
That candy bar marked my survival.

Snickers became both a quiet celebration and a personal offering, a way to tell my heart I saw it, cared for it, and still believed in the future.

There were no confetti moments, no one at the door applauding me for showing up to life when it felt unbearably heavy. But in that tiny act, I reminded myself: I'm still standing. I made it through. I matter.

I didn't realize then that I was writing a chapter that would one day carry the weight of an entire book. I only knew I needed something, anything, to anchor me in the belief that I was still worth the effort.

So yes, I remember the candy bar. Not because it filled my stomach, but because it fed my soul.

TABLE OF CONTENTS

Copyright ii
Forward iii
Prologue v
TABLE OF CONTENT vii
INTRODUCTION 1
Part I: The Girl Who Endured 4
Chapter 1: Dirt Roads and Summer Food Truck 5
Chapter 2: The Sprinkling Before the Struggle 23
Chapter 3: Dorm Room Assignment 40
Chapter 4: Dollars, Defiance, and Dignity 46
Chapter 5: The Exit and the Entry 51
Chapter 6: Boarding Room 58
Chapter 7: Purpose at the Bus Stop 68
Part II: Becoming While Breaking 80
Chapter 8: Just Enough for Now 81
Chapter 9: The Candy Bar Ritual 89
Chapter 10: When God Sees You 96
Chapter 11: Parking Lot Praise 106
Chapter 12: A Seat Worth Sitting In 114
Chapter 13: Closed Doors and Quiet Fears 121
Chapter 14: A Door Reopened 128

Part III: When Faith Gets Loud 134
Chapter 15: Destiny 135
Chapter 16: When the Ground Shakes 143
Chapter 17: A Letter of Peace 152
Chapter 19: The Gut Punch 165
Chapter 20: When They Choose Someone Else 169
Part IV: Delayed Does Not Mean Denied 176
Chapter 21: Out of the Shadow 177
Chapter 22: Don't Ignore the Sparks 183
Chapter 23: A Leader Is Born 188
Chapter 24: The Long Way Home 193
Chapter 25: Leaving to Live 198
Chapter 26: The Message I Found 203
Chapter 27: Answering Your Call 208
Chapter 28: When Critique Meets Calling 213
Part V: Stepping Into the Call 232
Chapter 29: Starting Something New 233
Chapter 30: God Restores Even the Smallest Wounds
.... 241
Chapter 31: Healed In Plain Sight 248
Chapter 32: God's Business Plan 252
Chapter 33: Retirement Was Obedience 255
The Power You Carry 258
Epilogue: She Still Matters 262
A Final Word from Donna 265
Special Acknowledgment 266

INTRODUCTION

T his Story Is Not Just My Story
By the time you finish this book, my prayer is that you feel seen, not because our stories are identical, but because your heart has found its reflection in mine.

You've already met me in a vulnerable place, in that quiet moment when a candy bar reminded me that I still mattered. But what you'll discover in the chapters ahead is that my story neither began nor ended there. Like many women, I have navigated a life shaped by the complex intersections of faith and fear, strength and sorrow, purpose and pain. I have walked through seasons when I didn't think I would make it. I have survived moments I once believed would break me. And I have stood in places where the only thing louder than my fear was the whisper of hope that refused to let go.

Present and Powerful is not about having it all figured out; it's about becoming who I already am. It's about the long, winding journey from survival to significance, from silence to sound, from shrinking to standing tall. It's about the girl who believed she'd never be enough and the woman who now knows she always was.

If you've ever felt like your story doesn't matter, if you've ever wondered whether you're too late, if you've ever questioned whether healing is still possible, this book is for you.

What you'll read here is raw and honest. I don't hide the complicated parts, because wholeness doesn't come from pretending things don't break us, it comes from standing in the truth of our healing.

These pages hold the lessons I've learned along the way, the unexpected detours that could have trapped me in place, and the whispered prayers no one else knew I was praying while I quietly unraveled. I talk about faith, not only as something I believe, but as something that carried me. I talk about leadership, not only in titles and promotions, but in the courage to lead myself first. I talk about ministry, not just from pulpits, but in classrooms, break rooms, and at kitchen tables where women find their way back to themselves.

This isn't just my testimony, it's an invitation. You may cry. You may breathe a little deeper. You may remember something you haven't let yourself feel in years. That's okay. That's healing. By the end of this book, my deepest hope is that you won't just remember my candy bar, you'll remember the lesson it carried for you. You'll remember yours, that small, sacred moment when you chose to hold on, when you decided to believe there was more.

And believe me, there is more.

Let's begin.

Part I: The Girl Who Endured

Foundations in the Fire

Before I ever understood the meaning of purpose, life was already shaping me for it. Family, poverty, and heartbreak marked my early years, each leaving its imprint. All of it became the groundwork for the woman who would emerge.

The lessons didn't arrive with fanfare. They showed up quietly, in the classroom, in the church pew, and in the steady resilience of my parents. The early part of my life wasn't anything you'd see on a highlight reel. Yet it was extraordinary in ways I couldn't grasp at the time, because everything I built later was rooted in those beginnings.

Chapter 1: Dirt Roads and Summer Food Truck

Growing up at the end of a dirt road in rural South Carolina, my world was shaped by the simple yet profound rhythms of family, faith, and community. My home, surrounded by leaning trees that seemed to touch the heavens, was more than just where I grew up; it was the birthplace of both resilience and dreams.

Our house kept a roof over our heads, though its wooden floors were so weathered and thin you could see the earth beneath them. They creaked under every step, holding the stories of generations. There was no central heating or air conditioning, no polished finishes, no decorative luxuries, and for many years, no indoor bathroom.

Instead, we used an outhouse, a small, weathered shed that stood like a quiet sentinel behind our home. Trips there in the cold, in the dark, or during summer rains were never pleasant, but they were a part of life, and we rarely complained.

We didn't have an indoor bathroom until I was nearly a teenager. My mother made it happen. When that bathroom was built, it felt like a milestone, a quiet yet profound shift that whispered change was possible, even if it arrived in slow drips. For her, it wasn't just about convenience; it was about dignity. It was her way of showing us that progress could be made, that no matter how long you live in a certain state, things can improve so long as you refuse to become content with lack.

Though we lacked material things, our home was whole. It brimmed with laughter, music, teaching moments, and love. My parents made sure we always knew we were cared for. We didn't wear the finest clothes or own the newest things, but we had each other. And that kind of love wrapped around us like a blanket, keeping us warm through the coldest nights and carrying us through the hardest days.

Education was everything in our household. My parents instilled in us the belief that learning could open doors, doors they never had the chance to walk through. Every day, they reminded us that while we might have grown up in a home where floorboards crumbled into dirt and the bathroom stood outside, our minds could build a future entirely different. The expectation was clear: we would excel in school. Our parents knew knowledge could carry us far beyond the boundaries of our zip code, and we embraced that expectation with pride.

We knew unconditional love, and that love gave us the courage to dream, to imagine more. To believe that one day we might live in a home where you couldn't see the ground beneath your feet, where the bathroom was just down the hall instead of across the yard. But even more than that, we understood that no matter how much our lives might change, we were to remain grounded in compassion, grace, and unshakable faith.

That house, its walls, floors, outhouse, and the dirt road leading to it, were never a symbol of lack. It was a place where my parents invested in us so deeply that the harvest still flourishes today.

As a young girl, the wide stretch of our dirt yard became my stage, a canvas where I painted dreams with every word and every melody. I crafted songs from the depths of my heart, barefoot, with warm sand sifting between my toes. I sang and spoke to the trees as though they were an audience holding its breath for my next note.

The rustling leaves responded like applause, a natural symphony urging me on. Those moments transported me from a child at play to a storyteller and teacher in the making. I was listening for the secrets of the wind, eager to learn the dreams whispered by the trees. As a young girl, the wide stretch of our dirt yard became my stage, a canvas where I painted dreams with every word and every melody. I crafted songs from the depths of my heart, barefoot, with warm sand sifting between my toes.

I sang and spoke to the trees as though they were an audience holding its breath for my next note. The rustling leaves responded like applause, a natural symphony urging me on. Those moments transported me from a child at play to a storyteller and teacher in the making. I was listening for the secrets of the wind, eager to learn the dreams whispered by the trees.

I remember clearly drawing a hopscotch grid in the dirt with a crooked stick, my fingers moving quickly to shape each imperfect square. Hopscotch was never just a way to pass the time; it was a passport to unknown and thrilling destinations. Those uneven lines became the map of dreams, leading me beyond poverty, each square a new chapter in the story I longed to live. As I leapt from one to the next, I imagined teaching the trees the art of balance and joy, their branches swaying gently as if trying to mirror my every move.

Every rustle of the leaves and every echo of my laughter nurtured my imagination, letting it stretch far beyond the boundaries of my yard. In those concerts and lessons, I planted seeds of creativity, seeds that would one day bloom into dreams of standing before thousands, sharing my story, and crafting songs that would resonate deep within the hearts of listeners. I often remember those moments as pure joy, a joy that became a roadmap for my imagination, guiding me beyond where I was, even when I didn't yet know how to read it.

The church was far more than a building to us. It was an atmosphere, a sacred space that became our spiritual training ground. St. Mark AME Church stood with quiet authority at the heart of our small community. Within its modest walls lived generations of prayers, praise, and unwavering purpose. And it was there, within those same walls, that I found my voice. First in trembling speeches, then in songs that slowly grew stronger.

My father wasn't just the choir director; he was the heartbeat of music in our community. His voice could fill the sanctuary and reach deep into every soul seated in the pews. He didn't just sing music; he breathed life into it. As choir director, he didn't merely wave his hands before the choir; he led with intention and conviction, guided by a deep understanding of music's power to heal and uplift the soul. He was also a gifted singer, leading his own quartet that rehearsed faithfully.

I remember sitting quietly during those rehearsals, soaking in the harmonies, the seamless blending of voices, and the patient starts and stops as they perfected their sound. The rhythm felt magical, like watching scattered notes weave themselves into something breathtaking.

We didn't just listen to the music. My siblings and I sang in the children's choir, proudly wearing our bright yellow robes. Wearing those robes made us feel important, set apart for something sacred. They swayed with our every movement, while underneath, our hearts beat in a thrilling mix of nerves and joy.

We also had microphones, and standing behind them was both thrilling and terrifying. They amplified not only our voices, but also our belief in what was possible. I remember the soft hum of the microphone before the service began, the cool weight of the metal in my hand, and the way my voice, unsure yet determined, filled the sanctuary. I may have been singing simply to pass the time or to be part of something, but each note was quietly revealing the presence of living my purpose.

Easter Sundays were among the most meaningful days we celebrated in church. I dressed in my Sunday best lace-trimmed socks, shiny shoes, and freshly pressed dresses, then stood before the congregation to deliver my Easter speech. I always memorized every line. The sanctuary would grow still, every eye fixed on me. I was scared, but I chose to speak anyway. My mother sat near the front, her eyes locked on mine, her face glowing with pride. It was her unwavering encouragement that gave me the courage to stand tall.

What I didn't realize then was that those Easter speeches were quietly laying the foundation for everything that would later manifest in my life. They were my first experiences standing before people instead of trees, holding their attention, and delivering a message that mattered. I was learning to use my voice, not just in pitch or tone, but in power and presence. It affirmed what I was beginning to believe, that it was okay to be seen, even if my knees were trembling.

Easter Sundays were more than a tradition; they were a transformation. Between the yellow robes, the choir microphones, the early morning rehearsals, and the proud eyes of my parents, I was being shaped spiritually, emotionally, and vocally. My father's gift for harmonies and directing, my mother's steady teaching and quiet strength, and the sound of worship filling our church were all planting seeds in me.

Seeds that would one day bloom on stages, in offices, and across social platforms. Seeds that would carry me through adversity, give birth to a business, and eventually grow into books and sermons.

It all began in that choir stand under my father's direction, draped in yellow robes, our hearts wide open. To this day, I carry the echoes of that music within me. The rhythm has shifted, but the melodies still remain.

Childhood, for all its wonder and innocence, was also when I first became aware of the deep ache of isolation.

That isolation was reinforced by feelings of being unworthy of kindness or consideration, along with the constant flood of exclusion in both the classroom and the playground. There is a particular kind of heartbreak in being surrounded by people yet feeling utterly alone. Children often don't understand that differences should invite acceptance, not rejection.

One of the differences that kept me apart from others was something I had no control over. I was born with strabismus, a condition in which the eyes do not align properly. What made my experience rare—and more complicated—was that I also have antimetropia. This means one of my eyes is nearsighted while the other is farsighted. Because of how the brain processes vision in such cases, I can only use one eye at a time to focus. As a child, you don't notice it in yourself. You learn to adapt, but others see. And that's when the difference becomes its own quiet burden.

I grew up knowing that when I looked at someone, they might not be sure where my gaze truly rested. Some kids laughed. Others asked blunt, insensitive questions. A few avoided me altogether. I tried to pretend it didn't bother me, but it did. I can still feel the sting of being "othered" for something I couldn't change—something I never asked for.

I quickly learned to mask my hurt with a smile, to laugh before anyone else could, and to shift my gaze or posture to make my difference less noticeable. I was uncomfortable, constantly managing the expectations of those around me, because I was just a little girl who wanted to be accepted. I wanted to be seen, but staring at me was not seeing me. Staring at me only magnified my powerlessness and deepened my fear that I would never be accepted.

Yet even in the hurt, something deeper was taking root: resilience, compassion, and empathy. I discovered these not in moments of comfort but by walking through the fire of stares and rejection. I was often judged before I was known, and that shaped me. Those experiences made me fiercely protective of anyone who was made to feel small or unworthy because of how they looked, spoke, or moved through the world.

Strabismus didn't just test my confidence; it shaped my character. It influenced how I entered a room and eventually taught me to lift my head high, even when my eyes didn't follow in perfect sync. It gave me a heart that could truly see people beyond their appearances, because for so long, I had yearned for someone to see me that way.

Over time, I realized that while I might never use both eyes together in perfect harmony, God was using this part of me for something far greater. My condition became a unique lens, both figuratively and literally, that allowed me to notice what others might miss. I saw the quiet girl in the corner, the child too afraid to speak, and the woman questioning her worth, because at one point in my life, I had been each of them.

It was not easy, but it was transformative.

Today, I use that part of my story not as a mark of shame, but as a bridge, a way to connect with those who have felt overlooked, misjudged, or dismissed. I advocate for kindness because I know the sharp edge of cruelty. I show up for people because I understand what it's like to feel unseen.

And I keep showing up, not despite my differences, but because of them.

Summers in our childhood carried a rhythm all their own. While other kids marked the season with beach trips or shiny new toys, for us, the highlight was always Vacation Bible School (VBS). In our community, VBS was more than a week of memorizing scriptures and filling tables with craft projects. It was an escape, a place where faith met physical need, where the spiritual nourishment of God's Word came alongside sandwiches, juice boxes, and the quiet assurance that we were cared for.

It began with a white-box food truck.

From our home on a dirt road in the low country of South Carolina, we could glimpse the highway through a veil of trees. Around the same time every day, my siblings and I would press our faces to the window, eyes wide with anticipation, waiting for that familiar white truck to appear. And then there it was, sliding into view like a quiet promise.

The moment we spotted it, we sprang into action, shouting that it was coming as we bolted inside to tell our mom. She would gather us quickly, and together we'd head to the church, trailing the truck as though it were part of a holy procession. For us, and for many children in our community, that truck was sacred. It meant full bellies and open doors. It meant care, even when school was out. The meals came through the Summer Food Service Program (SFSP), a state-supported initiative created to ensure children received nutritious meals when school cafeterias were closed. Recognizing the need in our community, my mom stepped up as a site supervisor for our church, transforming the sanctuary into a place of both physical and spiritual nourishment.

Some days, that lunch was the most substantial meal we had. The way my mom served the food with love, dignity, and unwavering consistency meant it never felt like charity. It felt like the heartbeat of a community in action.

The meals themselves were unforgettable. I remember holding a cold box of juice, its surface still dusted with tiny ice crystals. Even now, I can recall the joy of sipping that sweet juice in the heavy Southern heat. I savored every bite, every sip of juice and milk, because I understood their worth.

And there, at the center of it all, was my mom.

She didn't just organize the meals; she served them with grace and a smile. I watched her unlock the church doors, wipe down the tables, and welcome each child as if they were her own. She recognized the need in our community and didn't wait for someone else to act.

Instead, she partnered with the state, opened our church, and poured her time and heart into ensuring that children had what they needed and parents had one less burden to carry.

While she handed out sandwiches, she gave more than food; she offered peace, easing the quiet worries of many families. She showed us what it meant to serve without seeking recognition, to show up faithfully for others even while navigating her own struggles. She didn't have to define compassion; she embodied it.

While she handed out sandwiches, she gave more than food; she offered peace, easing the quiet worries of many families. She showed us what it meant to serve without seeking recognition, to show up faithfully for others even while navigating her own struggles. She didn't have to define compassion; she embodied it.

Under my mom's guidance, Vacation Bible School was more than just Bible verses and crafts. It became a model of holistic ministry, a place where children were nourished in every sense of the word. We memorized scripture in the same rooms where we ate lunch, learning that being the hands and feet of Jesus sometimes meant simply feeding a hungry child.

I didn't know it then, but those days spent in VBS and waiting for the food truck to rumble through the trees would stay with me forever. I watched my mother, saw the community unite, and felt nourished not only with food but also with love. Those experiences laid the foundation for my life and felt like a glimpse of my future. They taught me that true leadership is about presence, and that dignity and hope can be wrapped in a paper bag, filled with food, and handed across a table.

Leadership isn't always held by the one with the microphone; it's found in the one who sees the need and chooses to meet it. In that little church with a white box truck and a mother who believed in more, I learned to believe too. But the nourishment didn't stop at church.

During the school year, I was a recipient of free meals through the National School Lunch and Breakfast Programs, the same child nutrition system my mom partnered with during the summer. I remember clutching my blue meal ticket, the one that meant I didn't have to worry about eating during the school day. Others might have seen it as no big deal, but to me, that blue ticket meant I wouldn't have to sit hungry all day. I could focus on my work instead of a growling stomach and learn without the distraction of a hunger headache. I also remember the warm smiles of the cafeteria ladies who served those meals with kindness and love.

Time in the cafeteria wasn't just about the food. It offered comfort, consistency, and care. No matter how much or how little food was at home, I could count on that meal every school day. It helped build a sense of normalcy and dignity I didn't even realize I was carrying. Being fed meant I could focus and learn.

The best school meal I remember was spaghetti, a cinnamon roll, corn, and applesauce. Whoever came up with that combination should win an award. Even though I was food insecure, my taste buds had standards. Our teachers would stand over us, making sure we ate everything because they knew some of us had very little food at home. I had no problem cleaning my plate except when it came to beets. No matter how hungry I was, I could never eat them. So, when the teacher turned her back, I'd cut the round beets with my fork and hide them in my empty milk carton.

Despite the simplicity of our surroundings with creaking wooden floors that revealed the bare ground, and an outhouse out back before my mom built an indoor bathroom, my spirit was never small. My life was filled with love, faith, and the certainty that there had to be more.

Even with bare feet on dirt floors and humble meals stretched thin, I dreamed boldly. I'd lie under the vast southern sky, arms folded behind my head, imagining a future where our refrigerator was always full, where I could walk into a store and buy groceries without counting change, and where I held the keys to my own car, not someone else deciding where I could go. I didn't just want stability; I longed for purpose, autonomy, and impact.

I didn't wait until I had it all to start dreaming. I dreamed amid lack. In the front yard made of dirt and possibility, I made up songs, singing to the trees as if they were my audience. I directed choirs of leaves with my arms and spoke boldly to an audience of sky. I imagined myself on stages, in front of thousands, telling stories that lifted hearts and helped people remember who they are. Even when fear trembled inside me, especially on those Easter Sundays when I stood in front of our church with my speech memorized, I showed up anyway. Bold. Faithful. Becoming.

My mother and father gave me more than provisions; they gave me a vision of how things could be. Their sacrifices and belief in us taught us that our beginnings don't determine our future. My dad, leading the choir with a voice like strength wrapped in velvet, and my mom, teaching Sunday School, modeled a life of power.

So, the dirt roads, the homemade meals, the church as a symbol of stability, and the early mornings watching the white food truck roll by all became the sacred soil from which I grew into who I am. These experiences were not just nostalgic moments; they were lessons in perseverance, in seeing value intertwined with struggle, and in finding hope amid hardship.

I grew up surrounded by the message that we might not have everything, but we had each other, and that was enough to plant dreams that don't die with disappointment but rise again and again, watered by prayer, persistence, and purpose.

Those early experiences didn't just shape who I was; they carved the path toward who I was called to be. They revealed a truth that would become my life's anthem: my past or future does not define me. I am worthy now.

Looking back on those early years, dirt roads and yellow choir robes, juice boxes and makeshift stages under southern skies, I see how every detail was divinely woven into my life. None of my experiences were in vain: the challenges, the quiet joys, and even the moments of doubt. The situations I encountered painted a picture of grit and grace, shaping the woman I've become and the mission I now carry.

What once felt like a struggle became the soil from which my strength grew. Our creaking floors and the outhouse behind our home were not signs of lack; they were reminders of how rich we were in what mattered most: faith, family, and vision. I was never without. I was being prepared.

Now, as I step into this new season, I no longer see my past as something to overcome. I see it as the foundation beneath my feet, a launching pad for every step forward. Those early lessons spoken in Sunday School, sung in choir rehearsals, and whispered in late-night prayers became my compass. They remind me to love, to speak boldly, and to serve with empathy.

I carry with me the voices of those who once saw me, fed me, and believed in me, and the voice of a little girl who used to sing to trees and dream of standing before thousands. That girl still lives within me. She's no longer afraid to be seen. She's no longer waiting for someone to choose her. She has chosen herself.

I am a living testimony to God's restoring power, a woman who once received free school meals and later retired from leading the very program that provides meals at no cost to students statewide.

I am someone who once whispered prayers in lack and now boldly declares promises in faith.

Chapter 2: The Sprinkling Before the Struggle

When I was twelve, I stood at the altar of St. Mark AME Church, a child brimming with anticipation and uncertainty. I joined the church, knowing that getting sprinkled was part of the process. The sanctuary, with its timeworn pews and the kaleidoscope of stained-glass reflections, held a quiet stillness as I stood there. The reverend approached me, holding a bowl of water, and I felt the steady gaze of the congregation, the same people who had watched me grow, stumble, and now take this step. When the droplets of water touched my forehead, I flinched not from fear or the sensation of water, but from the weight of what the moment represented. I sensed it meant more than I could yet comprehend.

Sprinkling was my first outward step of faith, a symbol of belonging to something greater than myself. I stood there in my white dress, starched and pressed just right, a symbol of purity and tradition. Like many girls my age, I instinctively ducked as the water was sprinkled on my freshly styled curls, trying to keep them intact while still honoring the sacredness of the act. I felt the cool droplets fall across my face, and in that simple motion, countless others had experienced before me, I was marked by something I couldn't yet name.

As I stood there, blinking up at the reverend with water dripping from my hair, I was still a child full of questions. What did it mean to be baptized? Was I different now? Cleaner, holier, somehow more acceptable to God? Was this what commitment to Him was supposed to feel like? I didn't have the answers. I didn't understand the depth of the covenant or the weight of the faith journey ahead. But I tucked that moment into the back pocket of my heart, sensing it would mean more one day.

That white dress may have faded, the curls long undone, but that moment, the duck, the sprinkle, the unsure yet open heart was the beginning of something eternal.

By the time I reached adolescence, I had already spent years wrestling with my reflection. My strabismus made me stand out in ways I never asked for. I drew stares that lingered and whispers that traveled farther than the speaker ever intended. Beyond the teasing and side glances, something deeper settled in my spirit. I began to believe I was not enough, not pretty enough, interesting enough, or worthy enough. I felt I could never do enough to fit in.

It's one thing to hear cruel words from children and navigate them in real time. It's another thing to start believing those brutal words. How could anyone love me? How could I love myself?

The sense of unworthiness wasn't just about how I looked; it seeped into how I saw my potential, my place in the world, and even my right to be loved. I could smile on the outside, be the girl with good grades, the one who memorized her Easter speeches, but inside, there was an ache, a longing to be chosen. Not out of pity, but out of genuine desire.

It felt like a miracle when someone finally noticed me. I was in high school, just beginning to imagine a life beyond our dirt road and earth-exposing floor. My first boyfriend was six years older than me, confident and attentive. The attention he gave felt like sunlight warming hidden places. He called me beautiful words I had never heard applied to me. He told me I was special and offered gifts as gestures of affection. I didn't know how to interpret it all, but I thought maybe someone was finally seeing me.

What I didn't understand then was how powerful and how dangerous that hunger for connection could be when it wasn't anchored in self-worth. After spending so long feeling unseen, the first person to look your way can feel like salvation. Sometimes, what looks like love is only a mirror reflecting desperation.

When he said he loved me, I believed him.

I clung to those words as if they meant everything. No one had ever shown genuine interest in me. No one had gone out of their way to make me feel chosen. When you've been quietly starving for affection, affirmation, for someone to say, "You are enough," it doesn't take much to convince you.

My boyfriend gave me gifts, attention, and what I thought was protection. In return, I gave him my time, my trust, and eventually, my future. I spent all my free time with him and his family. His world became my orbit, slowly pulling me away from friendships and routines. In his world, I felt like I belonged no longer just the shy, unsure girl trying to shrink through school hallways, but someone seen and wanted. I told myself this was what love looked like, that devotion meant immersion, and closeness meant safety.

I didn't know how to ask questions or even what questions to ask. I didn't pause long enough to wonder what lay beneath the charm or the flattering words. The dream of being loved blurred the warnings that stood right in front of me: my boyfriend's need for control, the subtle comments that chipped away at my confidence, and the way he isolated me from others under the guise of protection. When you've waited your whole life to experience a relationship, red flags can easily look like roses.

And so, on February 14, 1990, at eighteen years old, I married him. I was still a senior in high school, still learning to balance books and locker combinations, still dreaming about college, and now, I was a wife.

At first, it felt like a fairy tale. I thought I had graduated early into womanhood. The girl who never imagined herself as the bride in the spotlight was now someone's partner. I dreamed of partnership, of growing together, of becoming the kind of couple that proves love can be healing. I honestly believed marriage would complete me, that all the insecurity and self-doubt would finally fade because I had someone to stand beside me. But love, real love, doesn't confuse you. It doesn't try to consume you or alter your reflection until you no longer recognize who's looking back in the mirror. And it certainly does not hit you.

The first time he hit me, the world seemed to slow down. My body froze while my mind raced. The room felt both too loud and too quiet. My heart pounded in disbelief, and my thoughts swirled with questions. How could the same hands that once held me try to destroy me? How could the same lips that whispered sweet nothings in my ear turn against me with rage? How could those hands that once held mine in affection now leave bruises behind?

When my husband first hit me across the face, it didn't just hurt my body; it fractured something deep inside me. The safety I had felt shattered, leaving me trapped in a fear I didn't have the tools to manage. He never raised his hand to me while we were dating.

I remember sitting in the aftermath, shocked, numb, and confused. I tried to make sense of it all. Maybe it was my fault. Maybe I said something wrong. Perhaps I triggered a bad day. Maybe, maybe, maybe. I tried to shrink myself even smaller to appease, to pacify, to please him, believing that if I could be a better wife, it would stop. That the love I had could somehow overpower the violence I had just endured.

He didn't stop abusing me. Slowly, a different kind of silence settled in, one that tried to convince me this was my fate, whispering that this was the price of being loved. The physical abuse came hand in hand with emotional torment, financial control, and isolation. Bit by bit, he separated me from my family. I smiled less and laughed even less. The girl who once gave Easter speeches and danced in VBS vanished. She was replaced by someone I barely recognized, quiet, fearful, constantly calculating how to avoid the next blow, the next insult, the next moment of rage.

There's a slow kind of death that happens when you lose your sense of self, when every decision is filtered through someone else's control, and the light inside you grows dimmer with each passing day. I used to look in the mirror and no longer see myself, just someone surviving.

I didn't know how to leave. I wasn't sure if I could leave, and I certainly didn't think I deserved better. The low self-esteem that started in childhood had grown into something larger, something heavier. I carried shame like a second skin. I thought, this is what happens when someone like me gets noticed. Feeling unworthy and being abused was the price I had to pay. Looking back now, I grieve for the young woman I was, not with shame, but with compassion.

I step back in time, kneel beside the younger version of myself, and take her trembling hands in mine. I look her in the eyes—the ones she always tried to hide and whisper the truth she was too weary to believe. Love is never supposed to hurt. Being chosen is not the same as being cherished. You don't have to shrink to someone else's standard so they can feel validated. You don't have to accept pain to feel like you matter.

I told her that love doesn't confuse, isolate, or silence. It doesn't demand that you trade your dreams for someone else's comfort. Real love never asks you to disappear.
I don't just grieve for her experiences; I honor her.

Even when the world told her she wasn't enough, even when the mirror reflected more doubt than dignity, even when her joy appeared bruised and her faith cracked, she kept going. She held on. She found flickers of light in the darkest places. She didn't give up dreaming, and she didn't let the worst moments define her. She bent and became flexible, and for that, I honor her with my whole heart. She was never weak. She was wounded. I am, because she persevered.

That little girl sprinkled at the altar, the one in the white dress, who ducked as water was gently poured on her head, who didn't quite understand what surrendering to God meant, she never left. She was still there, buried beneath heartbreak and the weight of silence, waiting for her moment to rise.

One day, she would return to the altar. Not because it was expected, or out of tradition or routine, but because her soul was parched and desperate for the living water that could cleanse what the world had caked on her. That first sprinkling marked the beginning. It would be her full baptism that became the claim of the reawakening, the sacred moment when God reminded me who I was.

Baptism was a moment of rising for me, not just out of water, but out of survival and shame. It was the beginning of a different kind of walk. Baptism allowed me to see myself in the fullness of who I was created to be, even while confined in my current situation. Before that rise, I had to descend into the valley.

I had to walk through the places where dreams felt distant and my voice seemed useless. I had to confront the lies that had become part of my identity, the ones that told me I was too broken, too damaged, too far gone.

I had to lose almost everything I clung to: my pride, my plans, and my illusion of control, so I could finally find the one thing that had been with me all along, myself, and more importantly, the God who never let go of me, even when I let go of myself.

Before I ever stepped onto a college campus, before I believed I could have a future different from my present, I got my first job. It was at McDonald's, on Hilton Head Island. I was proud not because it was glamorous, but because it was my first step toward a different future.

I walked over a mile in the dark to catch the bus. The morning sky was still black, and the chill in the air clung to my skin. I didn't mind the walk because my job meant something to me. It wasn't just about money; it was about hope. It was about stepping into something I could call my own. Standing at the bus stop with aching legs and a nervous stomach, I wondered if working at

McDonald's would be the start of a better life.

I still have my first paycheck stub. It wasn't much, but to me, it felt like a million dollars. I held it in my hands and let myself imagine all the little things I could finally buy: a new pair of shoes, a hot lunch, a bottle of scented lotion. For a moment, I felt grown, proud, and valuable.

That moment didn't last.

My husband made me cash the check and give him every dollar. He didn't want a portion; he wanted it all. I stood there feeling invisible, as if my work, my time, and my effort meant nothing. He never celebrated me or thanked me for contributing to the family. Instead, he took my money and reminded me I wasn't free.

From that moment on, every dollar I earned had to pass through him. If I wanted a snack, I had to ask. If I needed bus fare, I had to wait until he gave his approval. I was earning, but I had no access to it. I was trying, but I had no reward. It felt like being trapped in a story I didn't write, speaking lines I never wanted to say. My husband only picked me up on paydays.

I recall one Friday when I cashed my check and handed it to him. When we got home, I asked for bus fare for the next day. He became angry and yelled at me. Later, he came to me with the bus fare and told me he had to borrow it from our neighbor. I had given him my paycheck just hours before, yet now I felt like I'd embarrassed him because he had to ask for money to provide for me.

And yet, I kept showing up. I went to work. I walked in the dark. I rode that bus not because he told me to, but because deep down, I believed there had to be more. I didn't have words for it then, but now I can see I was building something. Quietly, painfully, I was learning that even if the money didn't stay in my hands, the dignity of working, of showing up, of hoping that was mine to keep.

I didn't tell anyone what I was going through. I didn't know how. I thought it was normal, or maybe I thought it was what I deserved. Being noticed came at a cost. That love, if you could call it that, meant shrinking, surrendering, and losing my voice.

Every time I walked to that bus stop, I focused on the dreams and outcomes I wanted for myself. I held onto the hope that one day I would cash a paycheck and use it however I wanted. That one day, I wouldn't need permission to treat myself to a meal or a moment of joy. That one day, my hard work would lead to freedom. Slowly, with one foot in front of the other, I moved forward.

The turmoil at home made me cling to education. School was the one place where I felt some control, where my efforts translated into tangible achievements. Excelling in school became my refuge, a sanctuary where the chaos of my personal life faded into the background. My dedication was born out of necessity. The structured routine of classes and assignments was familiar, a constant in a life where so much was unpredictable.

As a senior in high school, still working at McDonald's, I thought I had the job figured out. I showed up, worked hard, and kept my head down. Then one day, the owners pulled me aside. They had been watching me, maybe it was the way I always kept my drawer balanced, or how I connected with customers without even trying. Perhaps they saw something in me before I even saw it myself.

They made me an offer that, to a girl living in poverty, felt like a golden ticket. They told me I didn't need to go to college. They would pay to send me to management school and train me to be a store manager. My pay would increase, and my future would be set. Hearing these floods me with a rush of emotions. On the surface, it seemed like the answer to everything: a stable path, more money, recognition, and, let's be honest, validation. Someone saw me and believed I was worth investing in, and that touched something inside me. They made me an offer that, to a girl living in poverty, felt like a golden ticket. They told me I didn't need to go to college. They would pay to send me to management school and train me to be a store manager. My pay would increase, and my future would be set. Hearing these floods me with a rush of emotions. On the surface, it seemed like the answer to everything: a stable path, more money, recognition, and, let's be honest, validation. Someone saw me and believed I was worth investing in, and that touched something inside me.

As I let their words settle, a new thought began to rise.

If they saw this much in me, enough to want to groom me for leadership, what else might be waiting out there? What more could I become if I didn't settle for what was right in front of me, even if it looked good and safe?

After I retired, I sat in a McDonald's and reflected on my time working on Hilton Head Island:

I was eighteen years old. A senior in high school. Newly married. And I had just gotten my first job at McDonald's.

That first paycheck?

It felt like freedom. Power. Possibility.

For a young woman navigating physical, mental, and financial abuse behind closed doors, it was the first time I understood what it meant to earn something for myself.

I was still attending class, still smiling at work, still figuring out who I was in a world heavy with expectation and survival.

Then one day, my manager pulled me aside.

They asked me to go full-time, skip college, and enter a management training program.

They saw something in me. And for a moment, I saw it too.

It was tempting because when you're being torn apart in private, being seen in public feels like redemption.

I paused.

I needed the money, and I was honored.

But something inside me woke up and said, If they see this in me now, imagine what I'll discover if I keep going.

That's the moment that shifted my life.
Being seen by others is powerful, but seeing yourself is transformational.
McDonald's didn't just give me a paycheck; it gave me a front-row seat to see myself in a different light.
I was already leading and making people feel seen before I had a title, a degree, or a business card.
That's when I learned a truth I now bring into every boardroom, training, and executive coaching session: leadership isn't a title, it's a decision. Potential doesn't wait for permission. The workplace is often the first place people are truly seen, and what we do with that moment matters.
Today, I help leaders, entrepreneurs, and organizations recognize and nurture the very qualities my first job revealed in me: presence, purpose, and the power of being seen.

So yes, McDonald's was my first leadership classroom, the place where I learned to show up before I had the language, degrees, or certifications.
It's where someone took a chance on me, and where I learned to take a chance on myself.

Leadership sometimes starts behind a counter, with a headset, a smile, and a spark of belief.

To every decision-maker reading this: never underestimate where greatness begins. Because your ability to see someone might be the very thing that helps them see themselves and the world differently.

I was poor, yes. I was tired and unsure, but I wasn't driven by money. I had an unshakable sense that there was more for me that my journey might start at McDonald's, but it wasn't meant to end there.

So, I turned down the training opportunity.

I didn't tell my husband about the conversation. I knew he wouldn't understand and would probably pressure me to take it. My decision wasn't about income; it was about my future.

Deciding not to join McDonald's management team was a significant choice for someone who grew up in poverty. When I received my first paycheck, it was the most money I had ever made, so even considering turning down that opportunity was huge. I walked away from guaranteed income.

Graduating as Salutatorian of my high school was a testament to my desire to pursue possibilities. This milestone recognized my academic excellence and gave me hope, a sign that, through diligence and perseverance, I could carve out an unhindered future. Receiving a tuition scholarship to Clemson University was an opportunity I hadn't realized I needed. With that scholarship, I became one of the first members of my family to attend college. The path to this fresh start wasn't without obstacles. My husband's reluctance cast a shadow over what should have been a celebratory transition. I couldn't smile or feel happy about going to college. I offered to attend a local school, but he was concerned about how the community would view him. A week before the official move-in day, he dropped me off at a motel without ensuring I had a way to reach campus. This stark moment was a reminder of the control he had over me. That motel room became a symbol of my isolation, a physical manifestation of the emotional distance that had been growing between us.

In that solitude, I grappled with a whirlwind of emotions, including fear and uncertainty. That quiet also gave me a flicker of determination not to give up. I reached out to my Aunt Rebecca as an act of quiet rebellion, a step towards getting control over my life. My aunt's support, when she and her son came and got me, was a reflection of empathy and love at a time when I needed it. It underscored a lesson that while adversity might be a constant companion, so too is the potential for resilience and the presence of allies ready to help us navigate our darkest hours.

As I stepped onto Clemson's campus, I was not aware of the journey ahead. The challenges were far from over, but the horizon held promise of growth, self-discovery, and a future where I could be the architect of my destiny.

Chapter 3: Dorm Room Assignment

Often, when we are moving toward freedom, our leap can feel more like a fall.

Graduating as Salutatorian from Estill High School should have been a time of celebration filled with hope and expectation. I had worked hard, pushed past obstacles, and earned not just a diploma, but a full four-year tuition scholarship to Clemson University. Unsure how I would afford college, that scholarship was a huge relief. People were watching, cheering, and eagerly anticipating whether I would attend college, including my husband.

At the time, I didn't fully realize how much his pride shaped that moment. He didn't honestly want me to go to college. He also didn't want to be seen as the reason I stayed behind. So, he let me go—not because he believed in my future, but out of concern for his image. It was a permission granted reluctantly, and that would soon become heartbreakingly clear.

Instead of helping me move into my dorm like other families did with joy and prayer, he packed up my belongings a week early and drove me to a hotel. Not near campus. Not with a plan. Just a place to drop me off because he had made other plans for the actual move-in day. He left me there young, unsure, and alone, without even arranging how I would get to school.

That week in the motel was my first true experience of isolation during a major life transition. But God, as always, stepped in. I called my Aunt Rebecca in Summerville, and without hesitation, she and her son came to pick me up. They loved me back to safety. They promised to make sure I got to the dorms on move-in day, and just when I thought the moment had passed, my husband showed up. Whether out of guilt or a desire to save face, he insisted on taking me to school.

Once on campus, I was informed there weren't enough dorm rooms to accommodate all accepted students. My roommate and I were assigned to an overflow room on the fourth floor of a high-rise dorm. That overflow room was a converted closet, barely large enough for a bunk bed, a single dresser drawer, and two small desks.

I climbed the stairs with my heart racing, trying to stay positive and telling myself anything was better than returning to the abuse that had been my constant companion at home. When I arrived, my roommate was already there with her family, looking bewildered. She had taken the bottom bunk and the top drawer. I remember thinking I had never slept in a bunk bed, and as I looked up at the upper bunk, fear gripped me. I immediately imagined falling out.

We both stood there, stunned by the cramped space. We made small talk about how tight it was and hoped aloud that once the initial move-in rush settled, we might be reassigned to a proper room.

I set down a few things and went back to the car to get the rest. But when I returned less than ten minutes later, everything had changed. The bottom bunk was bare. Her drawer was empty. My roommate's name was crossed off the door. She was gone just like that. I never saw her again.

Suddenly, I had the room to myself. It no longer felt small and cramped; instead, it became a gift, a quiet oasis where I could think.

To me, Clemson was huge. I soon began searching for something I could connect with, something that felt like home. I found that connection in the Clemson University Gospel Choir. It was about more than music; it was about the people. The choir members welcomed me, and for the first time in a long time, I felt like I had found my place.

I looked forward to Wednesday night Bible Study and choir rehearsals. Week after week, I showed up hungry for peace, connection, and something solid amid the uncertainty in my life.

During one of those Bible studies, something inside me cracked. Emotions and memories seeped out, and a deep ache I had buried beneath smiles and busy schedules surfaced like a balloon finally releasing its air. The abuse I had endured didn't vanish just because I left home. It followed me in the fear I carried, the guilt whispering that I deserved it, and the shame convincing me I was both too much and not enough all at once.

One night after Bible Study, it all became too heavy to carry.

I walked into the elevator hallway on my dorm floor and knelt down. The carpet pressed hard against my knees, but I didn't notice the pain. The white fluorescent lights buzzed overhead, and the silence gripped my chest. I couldn't hold it in anymore. I broke. Tears spilled out with a force I didn't try to stop. I cried until I shook until the silence turned sacred, until the pain transformed into something deeper: a prayer.

There, in that elevator hallway, I surrendered my life to Christ. The moment was raw and honest. I was a bruised young woman trying to believe that healing was possible. I didn't know what it looked like. I didn't even know how to ask for it. But I knew I couldn't keep living like this.

So, I gave God everything: the fear, the hurt, the questions, the broken dreams. I didn't rise from that floor with a perfect plan or an angelic chorus, but I got up differently. I got up lighter. I got up braver. That moment wasn't a breakdown; it was a rebirth.

It was the night the girl in the white dress, sprinkled at the altar all those years ago, began to come alive again, not for anyone else, but for herself; for the purpose she was still learning to believe she carried; for the life she was still learning to know she deserved.

That surrender on the dorm floor wasn't the end of my struggle, but the beginning of a different kind of strength. I didn't stand up with all the answers. I didn't suddenly feel fearless or free. But I felt held, and that changed everything.

I still had to walk through hardship. Walking to class with tears barely dried from the night before. My circumstances hadn't changed in that moment; I was still married to my abuser and separated from the very people who loved me most. My pockets were light, my heart often heavy, and loneliness crept in like a shadow

I couldn't shake. But something in me shifted.

That night on the elevator floor was a turning point in my life. I stopped pretending I could carry my burden alone. I finally admitted I was tired of holding it together while falling apart on the inside. By releasing it all to God, I discovered a strength that didn't come from striving, but from surrender.

It didn't mean the road ahead would be smooth because it wasn't. Many days, I still cried myself to sleep, wondering how I would keep going. I still questioned my worth, feared the echo of my husband's voice in my mind, and wondered if healing was even possible for someone like me. But now, those questions were met with a quiet assurance: I was not alone. God had me.

Buried beneath the bruises, doubt, and fear, I began to believe I was made for more than my current circumstances. I learned that strength didn't always mean dominance. Strength means being okay with trying again. Sometimes, strength sits beside you in silence, offering nothing but presence. Sometimes, it rises slowly from the floor of a dorm room with tear-stained cheeks and a trembling heart ready to live one day at a time.

Chapter 4: Dollars, Defiance, and Dignity

College didn't just stretch me, it shook me. Coming from a small-town school where I had graduated as Salutatorian, I thought I knew everything I needed to live life. I had been celebrated, praised, and told I was smart. But the moment I got my first D at Clemson, all that praise felt like a lie.

I remember staring at that grade, stunned, embarrassed, ashamed. I thought high school had tricked me. Maybe I wasn't as smart as I believed, and the real world was showing me my place. For a brief moment, despair crushed me. I questioned my intelligence, my future, and my place at Clemson.

But I didn't let that feeling linger. I took a breath, wiped my eyes, and made a decision: I wouldn't let this define me. I belonged there.

I dug in, sought help, and changed how I studied, how I organized my time, and how I showed up for myself. I adjusted, adapted, and fought my way back. By my second year, the same girl who had felt defeated by a D was making the Dean's List.

But that wasn't the only change. In the midst of my academic transformation, I also began reimagining my purpose. When I first arrived at Clemson, my declared major was Mathematics Education. My high school math teacher had a profound influence on me. He saw potential in me when I didn't see it in myself. I wanted to be just like him, intelligent, impactful, and dependable. I also wanted stability. Math teachers were always in demand, and I thought that path would protect me from the lack I had grown up with.

As I moved through my coursework, something inside me kept stirring. Formulas didn't excite me. I was drawn instead to helping and understanding people. I spent time listening, supporting, and guiding others. Over time, I surrendered to a truth I had always known in the fiber of my being. I wasn't created to connect mathematical dots; I was created to connect emotional dots.

I reluctantly changed my major from math education to sociology and psychology. It was a move that felt both terrifying and liberating. I was letting go of the safe path, just as I had with the McDonald's opportunity, and stepping into the unknown. I believed God would order my steps on this college journey, and He did.

Financially, college was still a concern. Though I had a full scholarship covering tuition, it didn't cover everything. I had to take out student loans to make ends meet. And when those refund checks came, meant to cover books, supplies, and survival, my husband demanded I send them to him.

His voice was always firm, laced with that familiar control. The same voice that had taken my paychecks from McDonald's. The same voice that made me beg for bus fare after giving him every dollar I earned. But this time, something was different.
This time, I paused. That memory, the humiliation of having to ask for money after working hard, flashed through my mind like lightning. I remembered how small I had felt. How invisible. How worthless.

I said no. Not out loud. Not with a scream. But with a quiet, defiant decision. My husband wasn't getting all of it. I reasoned to myself that since we were married, I would send him enough to cover the cost of picking me up, but I was not sending him everything.
For the first time, I chose myself. I kept enough to survive the semester. Enough to breathe.

It might seem like a small moment, but for me, it was a revolution. That act of resistance was the first time I drew a boundary with him. It wasn't bold or dramatic, but it was mine. And it gave me the courage to start listening to my voice again.

During this time, I also began working on campus. I became a desk clerk and later, a resident assistant (RA). These jobs provided financial benefits I didn't have to give to anyone. Having a job gave me structure, a sense of community, and the feeling of belonging.

As an RA, I was responsible for mentoring students, managing conflicts, and creating a safe environment for others. It was a role I had never really had for myself during those years. It felt good to be needed, to lead, and to help others. It affirmed that supporting people was the reason I was created.

One of the first principles of the Bible I latched onto was tithing. Throughout my college journey, my tithing remained consistent. Giving to God was never negotiable for me. Whether my paycheck was $50 or $500, I tithed. It didn't matter that I was barely making it. I had made a promise to God. I knew that if I trusted Him with my soul, I could trust Him with my finances. He always provided.

Sometimes, the provision came through a random check from a friend. Sometimes through a free meal, and other times through unexpected favors from professors or bosses. He always made a way. Tithing wasn't a transaction; it was a matter of trust. It was me saying there's more coming, and I wouldn't always live like this. That obedience brought overflow, and it did. Not just financially, but spiritually, emotionally, and professionally.

College taught me more than theories and textbooks. It taught me how to believe in myself. It taught me how to say no and mean it. It taught me that setbacks aren't signs of failure; they're invitations to rise. It taught me that faith isn't loud, it's consistent. It taught me that dignity isn't something someone gives you; it's something you possess and decide to walk into.

Every time I held a paycheck. Every time, I kept what I needed. Every time I tithed before doing anything else. I was learning how to be me again, and this version of me, though still becoming, was rising higher every day.

Chapter 5: The Exit and the Entry

Graduation day arrived like a long-awaited sunrise, radiant, almost unreal, something I once feared I would never witness. The day was bright, beautiful, and tinged with quiet terror. I was deeply proud.

I had accomplished something that, by every statistical, emotional, and spiritual measure, once felt impossible. I had walked the halls of Clemson University, earned a place on the Dean's List, juggled on-campus jobs, and even changed my major to follow my heart, and now, I was walking away with a degree. A hard-won triumph no one could ever take from me.

Yet beneath that cap and gown was a young woman trembling inside, because I knew exactly what graduation meant. It meant no more dorm room to retreat to. No more crisp fall mornings walking to class. No more Gospel choir rehearsals or RA meetings to give my days structure. It meant going back home—and home meant facing my abusive husband.

Every summer during college, I returned to face the same abuse I had only temporarily escaped. The slaps. The controlling comments. The financial manipulation. The emotional whiplash of being called beautiful one day and worthless the next.

I endured those months because I knew August would come and with it, my escape back to school. I clung to the calendar as if it were my lifeline. But now, I had reached the season when autumn held no promise. There was no campus, only the house where I had learned to shrink myself into silence.

I returned and slipped back into the life I had left, working at McDonald's and struggling to breathe beneath the weight of a life that felt both too small and too painful to bear.
Then something shifted.
I applied for a job at a local bank, and by the grace of God, I got it. It felt like more than a paycheck; it was a window cracking open, just wide enough to let fresh air in. I dressed up every day, walked into that bank with purpose, and told myself, maybe this is where things turn around.

When payday came, I made a bold move. I told my husband I had opened a bank account. I explained to him calmly and clearly that I would tithe first because God came first. Then I would budget the rest and give him a portion. He looked at me as if I were speaking a foreign language. He couldn't understand why I would give so much to the church. He couldn't grasp that my tithe was my declaration of freedom.

It was my way of saying: God is my source, not this job. God is my strength, not him. And God is my provider, not a paycheck. I was beginning to believe that if I honored God, He would honor me; if I sowed in faith, even in fear, He would bring a harvest no one could steal.

Then, the day came. The day I had promised God I would leave if He let me live became one of my most decisive moments—a moment of desperate surrender. It happened on a long, lonely dirt road, flanked by endless rows of cornfields. The kind of place where no one would hear you scream. Where no one would know what had happened until it was too late.

One afternoon, my husband unexpectedly picked me up from the bus stop. From the moment I got in the car, he didn't say a word. Then something else unexpected happened, he drove past the road that led home. Instead of turning down our street, he kept going, turning instead onto a dirt road.

When he stopped the car, my stomach dropped hard. He spoke for the first time, ordering me to get out. I refused, and I made that clear. My refusal only fueled his anger. He yanked me from the car as I screamed and clung to the doorframe. My feet scraped against gravel, my body gone limp with fear. And there, on that dusty, secluded road, he beat me.

I lay on the ground breathless, broken, and afraid. Each blow blurred the line between this world and the next. I smelled the earth. I felt the fire of survival rising from a place so deep inside me, I hadn't known it existed.

That's when I made the promise. Lying there in the dirt, I whispered through tears, "God, if You let me survive this, I will leave. I will not come back. Just let me live." That prayer wasn't elegant or dressed in church language. It was raw. It was all I had left. And then I felt it.

Not a voice this time. Not a word but a warmth. A flicker. An ember. It burned in the pit of my belly, the faintest flame refusing to go out. Like God reaching into my fading spirit, reminding me I was still here. I am still worth it.

That ember didn't roar into a fire that night. But it didn't go out either. It stayed with me quietly burning beneath the bruises, beneath the fear, beneath the shame that tried to convince me it was all my fault. That ember was hope, and it was holy.

That was the day everything changed, not because I left that night, but because I decided to. When I finally got the chance, when the moment of escape opened like a crack in the wall, I ran through it with everything I had left, and I never looked back.

Starting over wasn't clean or easy; it was messy, raw, and often exhausting. My sister, God bless her, drove nearly two hours to pick me up. She and her husband welcomed me into their home in Columbia, South Carolina, giving me something I hadn't had in a long time—a safe place.

I didn't bring much with me, but what I carried was heavier than any suitcase. Fear. Shame. Worthlessness. Fatigue. And a thin thread of hope that this time, things would be different.

The first thing I wanted was to work. I'd always clung to the belief that if I could land a good job, everything else would fall into place. I thought transferring to the same bank I'd worked at on Hilton Head Island would be simple, but they didn't hire me, not even for a call center position. The rejection stung more than I expected. I wasn't asking for much; I just wanted a chance.

Still, I pressed on, determined to find a career job, something with stability, a future, maybe even benefits. In the meantime, I took whatever part-time work I could find. I flipped burgers in fast food joints, worked as a security guard, and even sold cemetery plots— anything that would bring in a few dollars. I rode the city bus for hours just to make a shift, then rode it back home, often after dark.

Job interviews were rare, and when they did happen, they almost always coincided with my scheduled workdays. I faced a choice: keep my part-time hours during the best daylight slots so I could at least keep some income, or risk it all for a shot at something better. The decision wore me down. I began to feel like I was always a step behind, as if the universe was confirming that I wasn't meant for more.

Then came the day I couldn't do it anymore. I sat on my sister's couch, my body aching from long hours of bus rides and burger flipping. I was emotionally worn, financially drained, and spiritually stretched thin. I had just missed yet another interview because of a work conflict, and frustration boiled over; it felt like I was moving backward.

I thought of my parents and the way they powered through when life was hard. I remembered my mom making sure we had clean clothes and love in our home, even when the refrigerator was nearly empty. I recalled my dad teaching us never to let our circumstances dictate our worth.

They had always told me I was intelligent, capable, and able to be anyone I wanted to be. For the first time in a long time, I believed them. So, I made a decision that defied all logic.
I quit my day job.

No savings. No job lined up. No guarantee that anything would work out. Reckless? Maybe. But it was the only path I saw to move forward. I chose to keep walking in faith, even with fear riding shotgun. I was done living like survival was my only option; it was time to start walking toward healing, even if I didn't know exactly where the road would lead.

That moment wasn't about a job; it was about pursuing something I felt deep in my soul. It was a declaration that I would not let what had happened to me dictate what came next. I didn't just want to escape my past; I wanted to build a future. And with shaking hands and a determined heart, I began again.

Starting over wasn't merely about leaving a toxic relationship. It was about stepping into the life God had been waiting for me to claim. One decision at a time, He began restoring everything I thought I had lost, starting with me.

Chapter 6: Boarding Room

After many months of staying with my sister and trying to figure out my life, we both knew it was time for me to branch out on my own. There was a certain comfort in being with her and her husband; they were family, and they loved me. She had opened her home to me during my lowest season without asking for anything in return.

She drove miles to rescue me, fed me, and gave me a place to begin again. But I knew I couldn't stay wrapped in that comfort forever. Healing, for me, required independence. I needed to stretch, to see if I could stand on my own two feet.

So, I began searching for something, anything that felt like a next step. I found a job where I could work at night. It wasn't glamorous, but it paid enough to cover some bills. More importantly, it freed my days for job applications and interviews. It was the only rhythm I could manage while rebuilding my life, piece by piece.

With the little money I had, I rented a room in a boarding house. The moment I saw it, I knew it wasn't ideal. The house was old; every floorboard groaned beneath the weight of years, and the air carried the scent of too many lives lived too close together. All the other tenants were men. There were no cheerful greetings when I walked in, no friendly smiles from neighbors, no front porch flowers, but it was what I could afford.

My room was a tiny corner of that chaotic house, but it was mine, a place where I could think and breathe. It had a private entrance and its own bathroom. That might not sound like much, but to me, it was everything. Privacy was a gift. That room was more than shelter; it became my refuge.

I was still carrying the emotional weight of everything I had left behind. Fear didn't vanish just because I changed addresses. Many nights, I lay in bed wondering how I'd gotten there, how my life had twisted so far from the path I once imagined. But every evening, I got up, rode the bicycle my sister had given me to work, came home, and applied for more jobs. I ate simple meals and sat in the quiet, letting my thoughts wander. And slowly, I started to breathe again.
Then came the phone.

When I moved in, I didn't have enough money to set up a phone line. Still, I plugged a phone into the wall, just to feel connected to the world. It sat there, silent and unconnected, a small, stubborn symbol of hope. Then one day, my sister surprised me. Quietly and without fanfare, she paid to have the phone line activated in my room. She never mentioned the bill.

The first time the phone rang, I picked up the receiver and burst into tears. Relief flooded me. Her gift reminded me that I was loved, that someone still believed I could rise, that my voice, no matter how shaky, deserved to be heard.

To some, it might have seemed small. To me, it was yet another sign that God was watching over me. The phone was proof that sometimes provision arrives in unexpected ways. This wasn't a miracle that parted the sea; it was a sister who heard my unspoken prayers and answered them with kindness. It reminded me that I wasn't alone, not in that house, and not in this fight to become who I was meant to be.

It was in that boarding room with the job I biked to every day, the phone line, and the private bathroom that I began to focus on what was possible. I didn't yet believe in everything, but I believed in something: in the slow, steady work of rebuilding, in the sacredness of small beginnings, in the quiet strength of a woman rising.

Even while my own life felt uncertain, messy, and often heavy, I felt a pull to serve others. I wasn't working a full-time job yet, but

I had a degree in sociology and a heart that yearned to make a difference. I had been taught that if you have a gift, you should use it. I knew I could listen, empathize, and show up, so I did.

I began volunteering at a local café that served meals to people experiencing homelessness or living in poverty. It wasn't fancy. It wasn't the kind of place you put on a polished résumé. There were no sparkling counters or matching volunteer t-shirts, just people with stories, with hunger, and with hearts that had seen far too much in life.

At first, I worked in the kitchen, helping prepare food and handing trays to guests. I stayed out of the way but made sure to contribute. Serving felt familiar; I had watched my mother feed children at church in the summers, and I had once been one of those children. Giving back now felt like an offering, a full-circle moment wrapped in uncertainty.

But something inside me stirred to do more. I asked the owner if I could learn more about the people who came in. I didn't just want to feed them, I wanted to know them. I began creating folders for each person, jotting down notes from our conversations. I treated every individual with the dignity they deserved, not as a number, not as a case, but as a person.

I helped them search for jobs, complete applications, and connect with shelters. I believed that if I could organize their paperwork, we could begin to bring order to their lives. With a sincere heart, I assumed it would be simple. In my mind, a résumé, a shelter, and a job would solve everything, but life rarely works that way.

I quickly learned that many of them didn't actually need a job. What they truly wanted was someone to talk to. Some didn't need to fill out housing forms at all. They needed someone to look them in the eye and say, "I see you." Some hadn't had a real conversation in days, weeks, or even months, and what they longed for most wasn't a sandwich; it was a human connection.

That little café became my classroom. And in that classroom, they taught me more than I could ever repay.

I learned that trauma doesn't simply visit us; it camps out, taking up residence. I was reminded that my own trauma had been a constant companion, looping in my mind like a song I couldn't turn off. I saw how abuse, addiction, shame, and mental illness tangled together into stories far too complex for simple solutions. So I stopped trying to fix anyone. Instead, I chose to simply sit with them.

We cried together, laughed over stories, and shared long silences. Some never even gave me their names, yet they shared their deepest concerns, and to me, that was holy ground. It reminded me of myself, because I knew what it felt like to be invisible in plain sight. I knew what it was to feel as though your value had an expiration date, and to wonder if anyone noticed you even had feelings.

Looking back, I realize those days in the café were profound. In that café, I watched dignity being restored in the quiet, in the choice to stay present, and in the willingness to truly see someone. I didn't know it then, but God was training me. Not for a job, but for a calling for ministry, for leadership, and for compassion rooted in lived experience rather than theory. In that place of service, I discovered that I was the one being served. My heart was being rewired, and my purpose was being refined. That's the thing about healing: it often finds you while you're helping someone else.

One of the deepest fears I carried throughout my life was the fear of not having enough money, enough peace, enough food. Food, especially, held a strange grip on my heart. There were days in my childhood, and even after college, when milk was scarce, and the cabinets seemed to echo with emptiness. I remember coming home from school to find that the only meal available was the cucumbers and tomatoes we'd grown. My mom would slice them into a bowl with vinegar, salt, and pepper. That simple dish was delicious, but it was born from necessity.

So, when I began volunteering at the café, I found comfort in more than the work. I found comfort in knowing I wouldn't go hungry.

The owner, a caterer, always had something simmering, baking, or cooling on the counters. I never had to ask; there was always a plate for me. I took it as kindness. I believed him when he said he saw potential in me. I believed him when he said I was like a daughter to him, someone worth guiding, protecting, and investing in. I needed to believe that. I had just left a violent marriage, walked away from the worst pain of my life, and was clinging to anything that looked like safety, stability, or hope.

So, I let my guard down. I let him help me. I let him encourage me. I let myself feel seen. But he wasn't who I thought he was. He allowed me to store my folders and notes in the upstairs space of the café, a makeshift office for my work with the unhoused. He praised my organization, my initiative, and my vision. I thought we were on the same side.

Then one night, after returning home to the boarding house from work, I found him in my room. I didn't know how he got in; he didn't have a key. It was late. I was startled. He said he was in trouble running from the police, scared, and needing a place to hide.

I was uncomfortable. Every part of me was on edge. But I didn't know how to say no. I was still learning what "no" sounded like in my own voice. I was still unlearning the belief that other people's needs came before my boundaries. I was still trying to be friendly, helpful, and understanding, even when everything inside me wanted to scream.

And while I was still trying to understand what was happening, everything changed. There were no warning signs. No slow advances. Just force. He took what was never his to take.

I remember lying still afterward, feeling as though my body had detached from my spirit so I could survive. My mind was loud and quiet all at once, screaming questions while going numb.

Why did he do that?
Why didn't I stop him?
Why didn't I see it coming?

I thought I was safe. I thought I was smarter than this.
At that moment, I didn't feel like a person. I felt like a possession, and worse, I felt ashamed for letting it happen, even though I had done nothing wrong. I didn't call the police. I didn't go to the hospital. I didn't even call my sister. I didn't know how to explain what I couldn't fully understand myself. I didn't want to be a burden. I didn't want to open my mouth only to have people question me instead of him.

So, I called a friend quietly, shakily. I told her I needed to leave, and she came to pick me up.

I stayed with her for a few days, barely speaking, barely eating. Then, because it was what I had always done, I got up. I put one foot in front of the other. I went back to my room and resumed my daily routine, which included continuing to volunteer at the café. I didn't look back.

Something inside me had shifted. I was tired of surviving. I was finally ready for a life that wouldn't require me to shrink, hide, or excuse other people's evil just so I could keep breathing. I didn't have a plan yet, but somewhere in the deepest, most wounded part of me,

I still believed God saw me. Even here. Even now. Even after this. I didn't know how to process the violation, so I told myself stories. I said it wasn't what it seemed. Maybe my attacker cared. Perhaps I had somehow allowed it because believing I had some control felt less painful than accepting I had none.

But my soul knew the truth. And I want to say this, gently and clearly, to the person who might be reading and nodding quietly through tears: It wasn't your fault. You didn't deserve it. You're still whole. You're still holy.

What he did to me didn't change who I was. It didn't remove God's hand from my life. It didn't cancel the call He had placed on me. It didn't unmake the woman I was.

That man took something from me that night, but he didn't get to define me. I refused to let that be the final word.

So, I kept showing up to serve others. I kept riding the bus. I kept believing that something better was yet to come, not because I felt powerful, but because deep inside me, a voice kept saying I was created for more than pain. So, I kept showing up to serve others. I kept riding the bus. I kept believing that something better was yet to come, not because I felt powerful, but because deep inside me, a voice kept saying I was created for more than pain.

Chapter 7: Purpose at the Bus Stop

But I wasn't ready to name it.

I wasn't ready to acknowledge what had happened to me for what it was: a violation, a betrayal, and manipulation.

Not again. Not after everything I had already survived. I had endured too much to admit that I had once more become a victim. So, I did what many of us do when we've experienced brokenness in quiet, hidden ways: I built a story around the pain. Not to lie, but to breathe.

Maybe he cared, I told myself. Perhaps he saw something in me. It could be a misunderstanding. Maybe I didn't say no loud enough, early enough, forcefully enough. Maybe I didn't fight hard enough. Maybe it was my fault.

I began shaping the story in my head into something I could tolerate, something less violating, less shameful. Admitting the whole truth that he had used me, controlled me, and discarded me felt like it would strip away what little strength I had left. I couldn't bear the weight of another scar. I was just beginning to believe I might matter, and now here I was again, reduced to silence.

So, I minimized it. I kept volunteering. I kept showing up. I worked beside him as if nothing had happened, as if I was okay, as if I wasn't crying myself to sleep or flinching at the sound of his voice. I tried to recast the narrative so it appeared we were simply two people doing good work, but I knew the truth. I knew I had been violated in the worst way by someone who would never apologize, someone who believed it was his right because of everything he had done for me.

He never cared for me. If he had, he would have protected me instead of preying on me. Maybe at one point I convinced myself he wanted a relationship, but as time passed, the truth became painfully clear: he didn't want me. He wanted power and control over me.

That realization was like standing in a familiar room and suddenly noticing every shadow. Every gesture, every compliment, every shared meal looked different in hindsight, sinister. It had never been about my well-being. It had always been about how close he could get without suspicion; how much he could take without being stopped. And once again, I hadn't stopped him.

That's when I learned a hard truth: survival is not the same as healing. And healing? Healing begins only when we tell the truth to ourselves, even if no one else is ready to hear it.

I no longer wanted to keep working odd jobs or pretending I was okay. I was exhausted emotionally, spiritually, and physically. The volunteer work at the café no longer felt like a calling; it felt like a nightmare I couldn't wake from. My dignity was gone, and I could feel the walls closing in.

I was no longer making enough money to pay my rent, and a decision had to be made. One day, my assailant suggested I go back to school. College would offer housing and meals. I had always dreamed of earning a master's degree, but not like this. Not as an escape route. Not because I needed a bed more than a syllabus.

Yet, that's exactly what it was: a chance to sleep in safety, a new address, and a reason to walk away from the café without confrontation.

So, I said yes. Just like that, God carved a path for me again right through an open door that looked nothing like deliverance. He gave me an exit from an abusive situation, disguised as an enrollment.

I gave up my boarding room, packed my things, and stepped into the unknown once more without answers, but with hope. This time, the space I entered would bring me peace. When I began the program, I didn't walk in as a student. I walked in as a survivor looking for shelter.

My mind wasn't on deadlines or discussion boards; it was still replaying what I had survived. I was still aching, still questioning.

But I was moving. And movement, no matter how slow or uncertain, is still grace. God didn't just call me to rebuild my life; He gave me a chance to believe in it again. In between classes, I applied for jobs. I was finally in a safe environment, no longer afraid of being followed or tiptoeing through someone else's rage. But safety didn't mean I had my life figured out. I needed more than peace, I needed a plan.

The clock was ticking. When the school year ended, so would my access to housing. The dorm room that had become my sanctuary would no longer be mine. I loved being back in school, the way learning sharpened my thinking and stirred something deep inside me I had almost forgotten. But love doesn't pay rent, and curiosity doesn't cover groceries. So, I pressed on. Every break between classes became a chance to send one more résumé, check one more listing, and whisper one more prayer.

The interview calls began coming in, each one carrying an impossible choice: attend class or go to the interview. Miss a lecture, or miss a chance to survive. Some days, I slipped into my best clearance-rack blouse and headed to job interviews, fully aware I'd fall behind in my coursework. Other days, I sat in class, trying to ignore the gnawing truth: I had no income, no backup plan, and nowhere to go once the semester ended.

I didn't miss classes out of indifference; I missed them because I was desperately trying to hold my life together. That was the part no one saw: the exhaustion of being both a student and a survivor, the quiet panic of knowing time was running out, and all I had to lean on was my faith and a few printed résumés.

Each day, I wrestled with the same question: work or class? There were nights when I cried over my textbooks, not because the material was too difficult, but because I didn't know how I would manage everything alone. I had never fought so hard just to keep my head above water. And in the midst of all that juggling, something unexpected was beginning to take shape.
I was building muscle, not just academic muscle or professional polish, but spiritual and emotional resilience. The kind that lets

you walk into an interview still shaking from a breakdown the night before and smile because you know you belong.

I began to realize I didn't just want a job; I wanted a career that aligned with the person I was becoming. I didn't want to slip back into survival mode; I wanted work that would allow me to thrive. So I kept going, kept studying, and kept applying, because giving up was never an option.

There are moments in life that feel like slow unraveling. You don't even realize you're spiraling until you're mid-spin, trying desperately to hold everything together.

That's where I was, somewhere between survival and surrender. I had escaped an abusive marriage and rebuilt fragments of my life from a boarding house room. I had volunteered my way into purpose, but even purpose comes with a cost, and I was running on empty.

I didn't have a full-time job. I didn't have a car or a driver's license. All I had was a growing sense that something had to change. I clung to school as a lifeline, enrolling in a master's program to stay both housed and hopeful. But I knew that eventually the semester would end, and when it did, without a job, I had no backup plan.

I applied for work nonstop, sending out applications with more faith than certainty, and hearing nothing in return. I told myself every "no" was just a setup for the "yes" that had my name on it.

Still, I couldn't ignore the truth without transportation, even the jobs I applied for felt out of reach. I had always assumed you needed a car before you could get a license, but something in me said, Start anyway. So, I enrolled in a driver's education course.

I didn't tell anyone at first. It felt too fragile, like speaking it aloud might break the dream. The driving school agreed to pick me up on campus for lessons, a blessing, since I had no way to get there otherwise. I couldn't afford many sessions, so I treated each one as if my future depended on it because it did. I studied harder than I had for anything in my life, and when test day came, I showed up praying that God would let me succeed.

I passed my driver's test on the first try. I still didn't have a car, but that small plastic card in my hand meant something profound. My license was more than permission to drive; it was proof that I was preparing for what I couldn't yet see. It was my declaration that I believed something better was possible. I wasn't going to wait for the doors to open before I started walking. I was already walking in faith toward the life I wanted.

Then, one day, the phone rang. The Richland County Department of Social Services had reviewed my application and wanted to schedule an interview. I gripped the phone like it might vanish, keeping my voice steady while my heart raced. As soon as I hung up, I got to work laying out my clothes, organizing my résumé, and mapping the bus route. I didn't have a car, but I had a bus pass and the unshakable belief that God was working things out.

On the day of the interview, I skipped class and boarded the city bus. Fear gripped me as I clutched the folder in my hands. My palms were damp, my thoughts a tangle of jumbled prayers. I asked God to go before me, to prepare the hearts of the interviewers to see that I could do the job.

I paused at the door of the building, feeling the weight of exhaustion, tired of being tired, tired of living in the in-between. But beneath that fatigue was something stronger: expectation. I wasn't walking into that interview alone. I carried with me the pieces of my past, the lessons I had learned, the tears I had shed, and the countless moments when I chose to keep going instead of giving up.

The interview was intense. I sat before a panel whose expressions gave nothing away. Their questions came fast, and I answered as best I could. I didn't have polished phrases or glittering credentials, but I had something different. I had lived this work. I wasn't just qualified on paper; I was qualified by pain, perseverance, and experience. I told them my truth. I let them see the woman behind the résumé.

Then, in April 1995, the call came. The Richland County Department of Social Services was offering me the position. I cried not just because it was a job in my major, but because it was a job where I could help people. It came with benefits, retirement, and a steady income. Most importantly, it aligned with my values, my calling, and the woman I was becoming.

Getting that job meant I wouldn't be homeless. It meant I could finally stop living in constant fear about how I would survive. My first assignment was processing and certifying food stamp applications, and that's when another divine full-circle moment unfolded.

I was now working in the same system that had once kept my siblings and me fed. As kids, we received free school meals and food stamps. Now, I was helping families like mine put food on their tables, the same system that gave my mother dignity when she stood in line so her children wouldn't go hungry. I was on the other side of the line, making sure people were treated with that same dignity.

Every application I reviewed, every story I heard, I handled with the care only someone who had lived it could give. I didn't see people as numbers; I saw them as souls because I had walked through that same fire.

The job didn't pay much, barely $1,300 a month, but for the first time in years, I had enough. A bus route carried me from campus to work and back. Rain or shine, heat or cold, I stood at that stop with purpose. I wasn't just commuting; each ride was a declaration: I'm doing this. I'm rebuilding my life, one step at a time.

A few months in, just before the school year ended, I found a one-bedroom upstairs apartment in a quiet complex. Moving in felt like breathing after holding my breath for far too long. Sometimes, I'd walk into the living room and stand there, letting the peace settle over me.

My furniture was a mix of pieces gifted by friends, a couch here, a coffee table there, each with a story. Each was a symbol of grace and of people who believed in me when I was still piecing myself back together. One of those friends would later become my husband.

I had a paycheck, a bed to sleep in, and a door that opened into possibility. It wasn't glamorous. Rent and utilities ate up nearly everything. I ate simple meals and had little beyond the basics, but I never went without. Somehow, I always had what I needed.

Though tired from long commutes and modest meals, I never complained. This wasn't a struggle; it was strength in its purest form. I was no longer fighting to survive the storm; I was standing in my own sunlight, faint as it may have been.

This apartment, this job, this season of scraping and striving, it was my beginning. An imperfect but beautiful beginning. No applause, no headlines, no spotlight moments. Just ordinary days stitched together with extraordinary determination.

It came with bus passes I guarded like gold and brown-bag lunches packed with intention, stretching every dollar and praying over every bite. It came with shoes worn thin from rainy walks to the bus stop and blouses ironed late into the night, hoping they'd hold up for just one more interview. It came with silence, heavy silence at night but also with prayers that rose through it like incense to heaven.

This season taught me that purpose doesn't always arrive with fireworks. Sometimes it looks like a daily routine, found in the quiet, yes, you give God when you're too tired to shout. It's in the bus stop before dawn, in the tears you wipe away in the bathroom at work, determined to keep going.

Faith doesn't always look like standing tall. Often, it's rising again and again in the face of uncertainty. I was working at the Department of Social Services, helping others apply for the same food stamps that once kept my family afloat. I saw mothers who reminded me of my mom and families doing the best they could. I wasn't just working a job; I was walking in my calling. From recipient to resource, from client to caseworker, from the other side of the desk to the one pulling up the chair. I had come full circle.

I had a job. I had a place to call home. I had a routine. I had a purpose even if it hadn't yet revealed itself, and, most importantly, I had hope. It wasn't everything, but for the girl who once cried on a dorm room floor and surrendered her broken pieces to God in a whisper, it was everything I needed.

Hope steadies your hands when your world still trembles. Hope allows you to believe that even this right here, right now, is a step toward something greater, and I was walking in it. One small mustard seed at a time.

Part II: Becoming While Breaking

The Hidden Work of Survival

There are seasons when survival feels like your only goal. These chapters hold the grit of my in-between space, where I was learning how to live while still carrying trauma, how to believe even as I was breaking. I didn't look like a woman in progress; I looked like a woman simply trying to hold on. Yet, in the heartbreak, the broken marriage, and the nights I cried myself to sleep, God was quietly rebuilding me behind the scenes.

Chapter 8: Just Enough for Now

Getting a job at DSS wasn't just a starting point in my career; it was a turning point. It was the moment when my past and my purpose met, and I began to see myself not merely as a survivor, but as someone being positioned to serve.

Because God doesn't waste our pain, He repurposes it. Every morning, as I walked to the bus stop, I reminded myself: I'm not just going to work; I'm walking into destiny.

When I received my first professional paycheck, I half-expected the clouds to part. Surely there would be more breathing room, enough to eat something other than ramen noodles, enough to finally catch my breath financially. I had a college degree now. I was working full-time for the state. I had crossed the bridge from barely surviving to supposedly making it.

But reality has a way of humbling even the most hopeful heart. The salary was the highest I had ever earned on paper, but that didn't mean much when rent, utilities, groceries, and bus fare claimed their portions without apology. There were no luxuries in those early pay periods, just numbers on a page that had to stretch. Paid twice a month, I quickly learned that budgeting wasn't optional; it was a non-negotiable survival skill.

The second paycheck of the month had to pull double duty, feeding me through the final days while holding enough in reserve to carry me into the next month. There was no safety net, no room for impulse, and no margin for error. I lived in a constant state of calculation, measuring out bus fare, meal portions, and hope.

Still, I didn't despise where I was. I leaned into it. That season taught me to see beyond lack to look not at what was missing, but at what was possible. I thought I had finally outgrown the fight for survival. I had a steady job, my own apartment, and for the first time in a long time, hope. I exhaled with relief, thinking, maybe now I can finally live without fear hovering over every dollar.
Then the deductions came: taxes, retirement, and insurance slices taken from my paycheck before it ever reached my hands. The reality of adulthood hit like a wave: even with a job, stability could still feel fragile.

Payday could still mean stretching pennies and praying the food lasted until the next deposit. The numbers didn't lie. The world could be brutal. But I had been through worse, and I refused to let the weight of reality crush the joy of the journey.

So, I made a choice. I chose to pause, to be present, to find the sacred in the struggle. I decided I would not despise my current situation. Even if I wasn't yet where I wanted to be, I could honor the process of becoming. I refused to believe this was the best it would ever be.

Every day, I reminded myself: This is a chapter, not the whole book. I am not my circumstances. I am walking through, not staying stuck.

My apartment, though modest, felt like a mansion to my soul. There was peace there. I remember walking through the space before the furniture arrived, running my hands along the walls, whispering to myself that I was safe. It wasn't just an apartment; it was proof.

Proof that prayers work. That surrender makes room for new beginnings. Proof that after everything, I was still standing.

The living room held a gifted couch that sagged slightly on the left side. The bedroom had a gently used mattress.

The kitchen shelves were stacked with mismatched dishes, and none of my curtains matched the paint on the walls. None of it mattered. Every item was treasured, and every inch of that space was soaked in hope. It wasn't decorated like a Pinterest board, but it was drenched in faith.

Most days, I ate ramen noodles like I did in college. Sometimes I elevated them, tossing in frozen vegetables or a boiled egg. Those meals reminded me that I might not have steak yet, but one day I would. I believed it. I lived like someone passing through, not settling in, and that belief shaped everything. I didn't look like someone stuck in poverty. I cooked like someone practicing for abundance. My meals weren't just food; they were declarations that I was going somewhere.

One afternoon, I sat cross-legged on the floor with a bowl in my lap, eating those noodles and looking around the space I had prayed for. Sunlight streamed through a thin curtain, and a quiet fulfillment washed over me. Not because I had "made it," but because I was making it.

Not because I had everything, but because I finally understood the beauty of just enough.

Just enough to eat. Just enough to rest. Just enough to breathe.

I knew this moment was holy in its own way. It wasn't polished or perfect, but it was mine. I had been shaped by seasons of survival, but this was different. This was a season of growth, quiet, tender, and steady. A season of becoming, carried on every bus ride, every bowl of ramen, and every whispered prayer over unpaid bills.

I had faith in God, and even more than that, I had faith that He was faithful. This wasn't the finish line; it was the foundation. I was learning how to be good to myself in small spaces so I could steward bigger spaces when they came. And they would come.

Because I knew then and still believe now that you don't wait until you're at the top to find joy. You learn to honor the *"just enough."* When you do, you're never truly empty; you're already on your way. That's the hard part for many of us. We are taught to chase abundance, to grind for more, to dismiss anything less than overflow.

But what I learned in my apartment was that *just enough* can still be holy. It can still teach discipline. It can still foster joy. It can still shape your character in ways that overflow never could.

I noticed something else: I wasn't the only one struggling. At work, I served clients every day who received food assistance: families, single mothers, senior citizens, and people with disabilities. I also began to realize that some of my coworkers, in entry-level roles just like mine, were applying for and receiving the very benefits we administered.

That awareness hit me hard. Here we were professionals. Educated. Employed. Doing everything "right" and still unable to get ahead. If I, with only myself to worry about, was cutting corners to make rent, what about the woman raising two children on a similar income? What about the man caring for his elderly parents without any family support?

I realized then that being employed didn't mean you had everything you needed. It was a truth that landed slowly, but deeply. I used to think that once you had a real job, a career with benefits, you had "made it." That you had escaped the reach of lack. But the longer I stayed in that position, the more I saw how untrue that was. Some of the people working beside me had been in the same role for decades. They were committed to serving their communities, yet still struggled to make ends meet, living paycheck to paycheck. Some skipped meals so their children could eat, still managing to scrape together enough for rent or prescriptions. It shook me, and it sparked something in me.

I started asking different questions, not just about systems, but about people. How do I help the working mother who doesn't qualify for assistance but can't afford childcare? How do I help the person who has never missed a day of work but can't afford to retire?

How do I help the woman like me, who has done all the right things and still feels like she's barely holding on? I wanted to help all people—not just those labeled "eligible," but anyone who needed to be reminded that they mattered, that they deserved better.

As I was learning, stability isn't just about income, it's about dignity. I wanted to be part of work that preserved that for others, even as I fought to maintain it for myself.

I could have settled. I could have told myself, this is good enough. You have a steady job, benefits, and a place to lay your head. Just be thankful. And I was thankful, but I wasn't finished.

The fire that had burned in me since those days on the dirt road, surrounded by cornfields, didn't let me get too comfortable. I wasn't chasing money; I was chasing meaning. I was chasing impact. Deep down, I knew I was capable of more, not because I was dissatisfied, but because I was designed to grow.

My paycheck didn't define me. It didn't set the ceiling for my potential. It was just one stop on the way to more.

I remember opening those pay stubs and, instead of resenting them, making a promise to them. I said that piece of paper was going to grow. It would not be the end of my story. I didn't despise my just enough. I honored it. I learned from it. I stewarded it. And I spoke to it: Don't get used to me, I'm just visiting.

I made peace with the ramen noodles, the quiet nights, and the checkbook scribbles. I found joy in small victories, paying my rent on time, considering opening a savings account, walking into my apartment, and flipping the light switch on with pride. I reminded myself often: This won't be forever. One day, I'd look back and honor this season.

So, I worked hard. I watched. I listened. I asked questions. I learned the systems, studied the procedures, and paid close attention to the people around me. I learned how things worked so that one day, I could lead where I once followed. And through it all, I held onto God and the truth that He never wastes a season, not even the ones wrapped in ramen, bus passes, and secondhand furniture.

When you are faithful with what you have, you are preparing your soul for more. And deep in my spirit, I knew that more was coming.

Chapter 9: The Candy Bar Ritual

One of the earliest lessons I learned as a child was that payday meant celebration. It wasn't just about the money; it was about the moments. When my dad got paid, we'd take a trip to the store for a Chick-O-Stick or a striped mint candy stick. I remember the joy of holding that candy in my hand as if it were gold. It wasn't expensive, and I could buy it with the twenty-five cents my dad gave me. But it meant we mattered. It meant he saw us. It meant that even if the world tried to tell us we weren't worthy, we still had reason to savor something sweet.

That truth stayed with me. So, years later, when I was living in my first apartment and barely making ends meet, I found myself returning to that same sacred rhythm.

I wasn't swimming in financial abundance. I had just enough that rent would clear, the lights would stay on, and I'd have bus fare to get to work. But there was nothing extra. Not for clothes, not for a restaurant meal, not for a movie ticket. When others talked about going out for the weekend, I stayed home. Still, I refused to let a paycheck pass without some kind of celebration. I had worked hard and didn't want to resent living in a cycle of work and bills with nothing else to look forward to.

On my way home from the bus stop on payday, I would step into the convenience store along the route. I'd scan the candy aisle as if I were selecting from a gourmet display. At first, I tried different kinds, but eventually, something about the Snickers bar began to feel like home. It had a bit of substance to it, a blend of chocolate, caramel, and peanuts that felt satisfying, almost like a small meal.

It was never just about the candy; it was about the moment. It was about not waiting until I had more to treat myself, as if I were worthy of joy. It was choosing, right then and there, to celebrate the woman I was becoming, even if the world hadn't started clapping yet.

After buying the candy, I took it home. Once inside my apartment, I'd take my time eating the Snickers. I closed the front door, kicked off my shoes, and sank onto the couch, sometimes sitting in silence, sometimes with tears streaming down my face. Then I would slowly unwrap the candy bar, peeling back the wrapper with care, as if it were a gift from heaven. I never rushed those moments. Each bite was a reminder that I had done well, hadn't given up, and had shown up. The empty wrapper tossed in the trash was proof that I kept going.

I remembered watching others celebrate payday their way, buying new outfits, planning weekends, and splurging on experiences. I didn't have that. I had my candy bar, and that meant everything because when you come from survival, even a candy bar can feel like a sign of safety.

It wasn't about the candy bar. It was about faith. About believing that just enough wasn't where I would stay, that this season wasn't the whole story. That God hadn't brought me through everything just to leave me sitting in a living room with mismatched dishes and frozen vegetables.

No, this was the middle. And in the middle, you praise with what you have. Provision doesn't look like overflow; it's what you do with what you have. I may not have all I want, but I'm not who I used to be. This candy bar? It's my praise and I meant it.

Every time I unwrapped that Snickers, I was sowing a seed of faith. I was telling my paycheck not to get used to me. I'm just visiting. I'm moving on. I'm building a life where you won't be the ceiling.

Even now, when I see a Snickers bar, I don't see a snack. I see survival. I see joy. I see worship. And I remember: I was worthy of sweetness even when life was salty. That candy bar wasn't just a treat; it was a reward. A moment of stillness. A declaration that even when things were tight, I was still worthy of something special. It may seem insignificant to someone else, but to me, it was an act of survival and worship.

I could have afforded the occasional indulgence, a new outfit, a dinner out, or a movie ticket if I had chosen to forgo something deeply sacred to me: tithing. I learned about tithing in college, when I first gave my life to Christ. Tithing was the first spiritual discipline I committed to, and from that moment, I resolved to honor God with my finances, regardless of my circumstances.

Initially, I tithed off my net income, giving ten percent of what remained after taxes and deductions. But as I grew in my faith and understanding of Scripture, I encountered the principle of first fruits. Proverbs 3:9 (NIV) states, "Honor the Lord with your wealth, with the first fruits of all your crops." I understood that to truly honor God, I needed to give from my gross income the full amount before any deductions. Initially, I tithed off my net income, giving ten percent of what remained after taxes and deductions. But as I grew in my faith and understanding of Scripture, I encountered the principle of first fruits. Proverbs 3:9 (NIV) states, "Honor the Lord with your wealth, with the first fruits of all your crops." I understood that to truly honor God, I needed to give from my gross income the full amount before any deductions.

This decision wasn't easy. Tithing off my gross income meant having even less money to stretch each month. But I believed God had sustained me and would continue to provide. Tithing was a declaration that I trusted Him with both my heart and my paycheck.

When I didn't have a church home, I stayed committed to tithing. I gave to whichever church I attended during that pay period, ensuring my first fruits were always returned to God. It wasn't about the amount; it was about the posture of my heart.

Most days, my meals were simple and straightforward. I ate tuna and eggs or ramen noodles with a few frozen vegetables. I never felt forsaken, even when my money didn't add up. My needs were met. God honored my faithfulness, providing in ways I couldn't have anticipated.

Tithing was more than a financial transaction; it was a form of worship. A tangible expression of my trust in God's provision. It reminded me that everything came from Him. During times of scarcity, I learned that abundance wasn't measured by my bank account but by the richness of my faith. As I continued to honor

God with my first fruits, He continued to bless me. Blessings weren't always material; they came in peace, purpose, and the assurance that He was with me every step of the way.

So, the Snickers ritual became more than self-care. It became a symbol of sacred rhythm, faith, obedience, reward, and rest. Every payday, I repeated the pattern, and over time, it began to change the way I saw myself.

I wasn't a victim of lack. I was a steward of provision. I wasn't someone scraping by; I was someone who honored every cent with intention. And more importantly, I didn't need to wait for more to experience joy. Joy was found in what was.

Looking back now, I see how those candy bar moments were teaching me about God's character, about His attention to detail and His delight in seeing His children enjoy even the simplest things. I didn't need a feast to prove His goodness. He was good at the bite-sized blessings, too.

That Snickers bar, whose meaning I never shared with anyone, became my communion. It reminded me I was still here. Still worthy. Still rising. I learned to celebrate the small things because I knew the day would come when I would sit at bigger tables, eat from fuller plates, and tell this story without bitterness. God had carried me because I trusted Him. And I had honored myself, even when no one else saw the cost.

Chapter 10: When God Sees You

There is a unique kind of ache that settles in when you're doing all the right things, and yet nothing seems to change. You tithe. You pray. You serve. You show up with your best, even when your best is a cotton dress from Walmart and a pair of shoes worn down to their last good mile. And still, you wonder if God sees you.

I was in that place. After settling into my first apartment and starting my job, I began searching for a church home. I wanted more than a place to attend service; I longed for a community where I could grow spiritually and continue walking out the faith that had carried me this far. A high school classmate recommended a church, and after visiting with a friend, I decided it was the right choice. Not flashy. Not perfect. But real, and that's what I needed.

Shortly after joining Haskell Heights First Baptist Church, one of the members learned where I lived. She wasn't in my exact complex, but close enough to offer me a ride on Sundays. That ride meant more than she knew. The church wasn't on a bus route, so I depended on friends to get there. When she offered to take me, my friends no longer had to go out of their way.

God was showing me, in small but profound ways, that He saw me. Every Sunday morning, I woke early, pressed my dress with care, and prepared for worship. I didn't have a closet full of church clothes, just a few decent pieces. One was a cotton floral dress from Walmart, my best church dress. It wasn't designer. It didn't have the tailored fit or polished sheen some of the other women wore. But I put that dress on like armor.

Even though I wanted a suit, it was all I could afford. I stood tall in that dress, knowing my presence in God's house was about alignment, not appearance.

My dress became a symbol of my commitment. Each time I wore it, I was reminded that I was choosing faith over fear and purpose over pride. That simple cotton dress carried my journey, my resilience, and my belief that God was guiding me.

At Haskell, I found more than sermons and songs. I found a community that embraced me and a place where I could serve. I joined ministries, attended Bible studies, and built lasting relationships. The church became my sanctuary, a place where I could lay down burdens and pick up hope.

Looking back, I realize that finding Haskell was a milestone in my journey. The welcoming environment reminded me that God's provision doesn't always come through grand gestures; more often, it comes in consistent ways that speak directly to our hearts.

I remember exactly where I used to sit in church on the left-hand side as you walked in. I didn't want to sit too close to the front where all eyes might fall on me, and I didn't want to fade into the very back either. So, I compromised, choosing a seat a little more than halfway up the aisle. Close enough to feel present. Far enough to feel safe.

The church was a comfortable size, with people everywhere dressed in their Sunday best, some carrying the weariness of the week, yet still showing up. There was something about the energy of the sanctuary, the expectancy in the air, that reminded me I was part of something bigger. I'd look toward the pulpit where the pastor and church leaders sat, and while they seemed far away in distance, they felt incredibly close because the Word they preached reached me exactly where I was.

I sat in those pews as if they were holy ground, pen in hand, notebook open. I wrote down every Scripture, every revelation, every word I thought might be God speaking to me through the sermon. I was hungry, not just for information, but for intimacy with Him. I didn't come to church to check a box; I came because my soul needed it. I needed direction. I needed peace. I needed to believe that the pain I had walked through wasn't wasted.

Make no mistake, life was still hard. I was stretching every paycheck, eating noodles and tuna more nights than not. I still walked to the bus stop in all kinds of weather, through blistering sun and pouring rain, to make it to work and back. But I did it. I showed up for my life. I showed up for God, because deep down, I believed He would show up for me, too.

That little corner of the sanctuary became my sacred space, my refuge, my classroom. It was there I learned to trust God, not for what He could give me, but simply because He is God. I believed that when the time was right, He would remember my faithfulness, not because I was perfect, but because I was present. Not because I had everything together, but because I kept showing up. That quiet trust, sitting on that pew in the middle of my process, became my anchor.

Church was not something I lived only on Sundays. Praise and worship became the rhythm of my week and the compass that steadied me when everything else felt uncertain. Beyond Sunday morning services, my friend and I made a point to attend Bible study. From the start, I knew I didn't just want to attend a church where the choir sang well or the preaching was polished. I wanted to be part of a church where I could grow, a place where the Word was broken down in a way I could understand, apply, and live out.

Those midweek services began in the sanctuary but eventually moved to the fellowship hall. The setting was smaller, more intimate. Fewer people, but more moments of insight. We'd sit in folding chairs, Bibles open, notes in hand, soaking in the richness of the Word.

Sometimes I left with more questions than answers, but they were the right kind of questions, the kind that made me search, wrestle, pray, and seek. It was a quiet kind of discipleship, a steadying presence that reached into the most complex parts of my life and reminded me.

I wasn't alone. Then, on an ordinary day, God reminded me again in a way that left me speechless.
I went to check the mail, expecting the usual bills, flyers, maybe a coupon or two. Tucked among the envelopes was something different, a handwritten note from a friend I hadn't spoken to in a while. Inside was a check.

It wasn't a significant amount, not enough to solve everything or erase the stretching I'd been doing, but it was enough to touch something more profound than my wallet. It touched my heart.

When I spoke with her, she said God had laid it on her heart to send the money to me and reminded me that she loved me. I stood on the steps outside my apartment and wept. God had heard me. He had seen me, not just the outer version who smiled, showed up to work, and sat in church, but the me who gave her tithe even when it meant I might not buy meat that week. I was the one who went to Bible study hungry for more than just understanding. The me who pressed her floral Walmart dress on Sunday mornings, praying to one day own a proper church suit.

I was the one who sometimes questioned if God truly noticed her quiet sacrifices.

That check said what no sermon had yet captured: I was not forgotten. It was like God was saying, "He's watching and sees the moments I honor Him in private. He sees the times I choose faith when fear would have been easier. He sees my desire to grow, to serve, to become, and He's with me."

That envelope didn't change everything about my circumstances, but it shifted something inside me. It reminded me that every seed I planted, every tithe, every prayer, every moment spent in the Word was not in vain.

I was seen, and being seen by God was more than enough. Little by little, He kept confirming that. Over time, I discovered two of my coworkers lived in the same apartment complex. On days when they saw me walking or didn't have other plans, they would offer me rides to work. It wasn't every day, but when it happened, I knew it was a blessing. These rides saved me from walking and helped stretch my bus fare. They shortened my commute and made the day feel a little lighter. I saw these moments as divine interventions, reminders that God's provision often comes through people who don't realize they're being used. I was careful not to impose, always mindful of not wearing out my welcome.

Without a car, my daily routine meant walking about a mile to and from the bus stop, whether the sun was blazing or the rain was pouring. I never complained. I prepared the night before, packing my lunch, laying out my clothes, and giving myself extra time. With every step, I whispered reminders to my soul: This is temporary. God sees me. Keep going.

I had my driver's license, but no car. Earning that license took determination and enough lessons to master driving. That little card with my picture on it became a sign of hope. Whenever the bus passed a car dealership, I'd peer through the window, imagining the day I'd drive off the lot. I didn't have the credit or cash, but I had faith that one day I would drive a car.

It wasn't just hope; it was belief. Not just in my thoughts or dreams, but in the deep-down place that knew God was able, even if I had no idea how it would happen. My credit was wrecked. I didn't have money saved. Still, over time, I received modest raises and promotions at work enough to consider affording a small car payment. The numbers still didn't add up, and the practical voices in my life might have said, It's not the right time. But I wasn't living by sight. I was walking by faith.

So, I began doing something that might have looked foolish to anyone watching. Every morning, before leaving my apartment, I walked to an empty parking space just outside my building. In my heart, that space was already taken. I had claimed it by faith as the place where my future car would one day sit.

I would step into that space as if I were getting into a vehicle, reach my hands into the air as if gripping a steering wheel, then walk backward, pretending to reverse out of the spot. I even glanced over my shoulder, checking for oncoming traffic. I could feel the weight of a seatbelt that wasn't there and hear the quiet hum of an engine only my ears could imagine. I'd turn, walk forward a few paces, and smile to myself as my feet became the wheels of the car. Those walks were more than movement; they were a declaration.

I did it every morning in scattered rain, scorching sun, and bone-chilling cold when my hands were tucked inside thin gloves. Whether I was walking to the bus stop or heading next door to catch a ride with a coworker, I never skipped walking backward out of that parking space. It wasn't superstition or routine. It was alignment. My body, mind, and spirit agreed on what I knew God was preparing.

I wasn't waiting on a miracle; I was walking in preparation for it. That empty parking space reminded me that faith isn't passive. Faith is active. It shows up before the blessing, moves as if the promise is already kept, and thanks God while you're still on foot. Every time I stood in that space, I didn't just see asphalt, I saw a glimpse of glory.

Those moments were my declaration: I see where I am, but I also see where I'm going. It was my way of letting heaven know I was ready. My faith wasn't waiting for circumstances to line up; it was already moving forward, even if my feet were still walking to the bus stop. And God honored that.

The truth is, faith doesn't always look like fire from heaven. Sometimes it looks like a floral dress and an envelope delivered in the mail. Sometimes it sounds like the rustling of grocery bags filled with dollar-store cans and clearance pasta. Sometimes it walks a mile to the bus stop without grumbling and waves goodbye to coworkers with cars, knowing your turn is coming.

Sometimes faith is just showing up, and sometimes, it's backing out of a driveway in an invisible car. Every time I did, I felt Him smile, because God sees and He remembers.

Chapter 11: Parking Lot Praise

When you don't have a car, each day begins before sunrise and seems to stretch endlessly. Some mornings, the wind sliced through my coat like paper; other days, rain whipped sideways so hard it stung my skin. Waiting for better weather simply wasn't an option. There were no Ubers back then, and a cab was out of the question.

Occasionally, a kind neighbor or coworker offered me a ride, especially in brutal weather, but it was never something I could rely on. I was always grateful when it happened, but most days it was just me, my determination, and my aching feet.

The bus stop sat about a mile from my apartment, the same distance I'd walked years earlier to get to work on Hilton Head Island. A mile might not sound far, but in the predawn dark—

through puddles, up hills, and across busy roads in worn-out shoes, it could feel like forever. Still, I walked no matter what.

I refused to give myself an excuse. I reminded myself that every day I got up, I was one step closer to better. I wasn't walking just to get to work. I was walking toward a future I knew could take many forms, a future built on stability. Toward the life I'd been praying for since I first set foot on Clemson's campus years earlier.

I was tired of rain-soaked socks. I huddled under bus shelters with strangers as my fingers stiffened in the cold. I was tired of trudging home in the brutal summer heat, my clothes clinging to my skin. I was tired of watching others drive into work while I showed up with sweat on my forehead or rain dripping from my sleeves.

I had a driver's license. I had steady work. What I didn't have was money for a down payment, and my credit score wasn't winning anyone over, but I had faith. A ridiculous, persistent, bold faith that told me to try anyway.

So, I tried. I began visiting car dealerships, big and small. Every time I stepped onto a lot, I squared my shoulders, wore my brightest smile, and told myself I belonged there. Not because I had money or approval, but because I believed I had the right to dream. I had the right to ask, and if God had a car for me, it was only a matter of time before I found it.

Being a young woman stepping onto a car lot alone was... an experience. I was either ignored or treated as if I were wasting their time. Some salespeople barely looked up from their desks. Others gave me that pitying smile that silently said, there's no way she can afford anything here. But I refused to let their assumptions define me. I held my head high, introduced myself, and asked about what was available.

I wasn't asking for a miracle; I was simply showing up where one might find me.

One day, near where I worked, a sleek, shiny used car caught my eye, parked at the edge of a dealership lot. It was exactly the kind of car that made you feel like somebody. I walked over and checked the price tag. To my surprise, it fell within my monthly budget.

I felt my prayers inching closer to being answered. I felt it deep in my spirit, that quiet assurance when heart and heaven align. The car was mispriced, and the salesman told me they would honor the sticker price. Sleek and well-maintained, it sat near the front of the lot as if waiting just for me.

This had to be the car I'd imagined every morning while pretending to back out of that spot; the one I believed God would provide.

The salesman approached, puzzled but polite. "This price isn't right," he muttered, double-checking the mileage. "It should be a few thousand higher." My heart fluttered as he continued, "But since it's on the sticker, we have to honor it."

And just like that, hope surged through me like electricity. I lit up, practically glowing with anticipation.

I knew what it meant in the pit of my stomach, the stirring of my soul. That car, sitting on the edge of the lot, felt like mine the moment I'd been waiting for.

The salesman and I sat down to go through the paperwork. Everything moved so quickly that I could barely keep up. My hands trembled as I reached for the pen. Each form felt like another stepping stone toward the promise I had been walking toward for so long.

I had already pictured myself in that car, driving to work with worship music filling the air, pulling up to church early, stepping inside without rain-soaked shoes or wind-whipped hair. I imagined carrying groceries without mapping out bus transfers. This wasn't about convenience. This was about freedom. This was about faith becoming something I could touch.

Then came the question I had quietly dreaded, even as I prayed it might somehow be skipped. The salesman asked how much I had for a down payment. My smile faltered just for a second. I met his gaze, took a steadying breath, and spoke the humbling truth: I had no money for a down payment.

He didn't scoff or shame me; he simply nodded and stepped away to run my credit. Then came the news I had feared. He delivered it gently, but it landed hard: I wasn't qualified for a loan without a down payment.

I nodded, swallowing the lump rising in my throat. I shook his hand, thanked him for his time, and tried to hide the tremble in my voice. I refused to cry in that moment. I didn't want to show the disappointment pressing against my chest like a weight. But as I stepped out of the dealership, I felt it rising not just sadness, but clarity.

That man might have seen me as desperate. He might have even felt relieved that I didn't qualify, so they could raise the price and make a bigger sale, but I didn't walk away bitter.

I walked away believing. Deep in my bones, I knew that if that car was meant for me, nothing, not my credit, the cost, or the lack of a down payment, could keep it from me. And if it wasn't meant for me, then something better was waiting. Yes, my faith was like that.

I had walked too far with God to start doubting Him now. I had worshiped Him with bus fare in my purse and ramen in my pantry. I had praised Him in a cotton dress, dreaming of a tailored church suit. I had tithed off my gross income, leaving barely enough for groceries. My faith was battle-tested; this was just another step on the journey.

So, I didn't let that "no" stop me. I lifted my head as I caught the bus home. I moved a little slower but no less steady. The promise hadn't arrived that day, but I believed it would, and I would be ready. I continued walking backward out of my parking space each morning, believing that one day my faith would become sight. Each step was a declaration of trust, a silent prayer that God would provide.

One day, during my lunch break, I noticed a small used car lot a short distance from my job. It wasn't flashy, no giant balloons, no swarm of salespeople. The owner ran the place himself, with a modest lineup of vehicles on a gravel lot. Something about him felt approachable and genuine.

I decided to stop by after work to see if financing was possible. The owner greeted me warmly, a stark contrast to the high-pressure salespeople I'd met before. I took a deep breath and laid it all out for him.

I told him I didn't have a down payment and that my credit wasn't good. I made sure he knew I had a steady job, though. He studied me for a moment, then smiled and said he would see if he could work something out.

To my amazement, he didn't dismiss me. Instead, he walked me through different financing options. My heart pounded the entire time. I had been turned away from another dealership less than half a mile from here, yet I pressed on. Against the odds I had already faced, the owner of this lot helped me buy a car.

Before I knew it, he was handing me the keys to a used Ford. I slid into the driver's seat, my hands trembling, eyes brimming with tears. I couldn't drive off just yet. I needed a moment to take in what had just happened.

This was proof of unwavering faith, a tangible answer to countless prayers, a reminder that God sees, hears, and provides. When I finally drove off the lot, I whispered a prayer of gratitude. God had done it.

I had walked by faith mile after mile, day after day. I had spoken life into an empty parking space. I had refused to stop believing, and now I was driving.

When I pulled into my apartment complex, I turned into the very spot I had backed out of on foot for months in faith. I sat there in stillness.

This time, I wasn't pretending. This time, I wasn't practicing. This time, I was praising. I leaned my head back against the headrest and wept in worship. God had honored the prayers, the walks, the silent tears, the tithed dollars, the noodle dinners, the obedience, and the waiting.

It wasn't just about a car. It was about evidence. Evidence that God sees. Evidence that faith moves mountains. Evidence that when you keep showing up, even when no one else understands, heaven does, and heaven responds.

Chapter 12: A Seat Worth Sitting In

The day I paid off my first car wasn't about checking something off a list. I held the title in my hand like a weathered victory flag. My car was paid off, and that title wasn't just a piece of paper; it was proof that God honors what you surrender.

Each payment I made was an act of faith. It wasn't always easy. There were months when money was tight, when an unexpected bill or expense threatened to derail me, but I still made those payments. My car wasn't just transportation; it was a testament. It was the vision I had carried through those mornings standing in an empty parking space, bracing against the rain and cold, pretending to back out and drive to work.

I remember the day I made the final payment. I stepped out onto my apartment balcony and looked down at that same parking space, the one I used to point to with hope in my eyes and trembling faith in my heart. For months, my feet had been my wheels. I had imagined what it would feel like to reverse out of that spot in my own car. Now, that very space held the fulfillment of a promise. I no longer had to pretend a vehicle was there.

There it was, my car, basking in the sunlight as if it knew this was its destination, as if it understood it was more than just metal and tires. It stood ready to testify to God's provision. I smiled, tears slipping down my cheeks, not from sadness, but from awe. When you've walked the kind of path I've walked and prayed the kinds of prayers I've prayed, moments like this don't just pass by; they take root in your spirit.

Driving to work and church became something holy. I no longer had to rise before dawn to make the long walk to the bus stop or negotiate rides during thunderstorms. I didn't arrive drenched from rain or weary before the day even began. My mornings found rhythm. I turned the ignition with a whisper of gratitude. I watched the scenery change behind a windshield instead of through a bus window. Every mile was laced with praise.

I remembered the cold mornings when my fingers stung and my scarf barely kept the wind out. I remembered the humid days when my clothes clung to my back before I arrived home in the afternoon. I remembered canceled buses, missed connections, and long walks that tested my endurance. And I remembered sitting at the stop, wondering if God saw me.

He did. Now, when I drove into the church parking lot in that same cotton Walmart dress, I stepped out not as someone barely making it, but as someone marked by provision. There was confidence in my walk, not because of the car, but because of the God who had carried me to it. The dress was the same. But I wasn't.
And that's what God does.

He changes the driver before He changes the ride. He builds you in the walking season so you'll know how to drive when the time comes. He meets you in the middle of your lack, so you never mistake the blessing for the source of your strength.

Each time I drove, the drive reminded me that I knew this day would come. I had lived long enough to see this promise fulfilled, and if this day could come, so could the others I was still praying for. This wasn't the end. It was evidence. I knew, deep in my spirit, that because this had come to pass, the others could too.

I kept driving. Kept praising. Kept becoming. That season of my life felt like proof that God wasn't just responding to my needs; He was preparing me to hold more. I was learning that ownership wasn't only about material things; it was about stewardship. It was about showing God; He could trust me with small beginnings, so He could trust me with greater things down the road.

With a car finally parked in the space I used to walk out of by faith, I stepped into a new season, a season filled with gratitude and greater responsibility. For the first time, I had reliable transportation, and that small piece of independence shifted how I viewed everything else. I began reflecting more intentionally on how I managed my finances. I still had dreams stirring in my heart, and I wanted to ensure I was making wise decisions for the future.

That meant rethinking how I spent my money. I had come far from the girl who scraped by to pay rent and afford bus fare. With more resources came the need to steward better. Rent remained one of my most significant expenses, and while I was grateful for the peace and privacy of my apartment, I knew saving money could open the door to the next phase of my journey.

That's when the idea of a roommate entered the picture. I didn't take the decision lightly. I had fought hard for my independence and my own space, but I wasn't afraid of transition anymore. I had learned that when things shift, it's not always a sign of loss—it can be a sign of forward movement. So, when someone from my church mentioned another woman looking for a roommate, I paused and prayed for guidance. Moving in with her felt right.

She loved God. I loved God. We respected each other's space and shared values, and the arrangement provided everything I needed: a private bedroom, my own bathroom, and shared access to the kitchen and living room. More than that, it offered peace. It didn't feel like a step back; it felt like a bridge, a wise, God-orchestrated path to something greater.

That living arrangement became a season of joy and growth. My roommate and I encouraged each other, and I felt supported financially, emotionally, and spiritually. The same person who had helped me move into my very first apartment also helped me move into this one. Over time, we had been growing closer, slowly building a foundation of friendship. He had witnessed pieces of my journey. He knew about the early mornings, the hard work, and the dreams in my heart. And one day, he proposed.

We began looking for places together, planning with both excitement and care. He moved in ahead of the wedding so everything would be ready, and I cherished that season of preparation. I remember walking through the empty rooms, imagining the life we would build there.

On March 27, 1999, we got married a day wrapped in sacred vows, gentle tears, and joy. The wedding wasn't extravagant, but it was everything I needed. I was surrounded by my parents and by people who had witnessed my journey from struggle to strength. I stood at that altar not just as a bride but as a woman remade.

Within two years, we were blessed with a son, a beautiful, bright-eyed reminder that God doesn't just rescue, He rebuilds. He doesn't just heal, He establishes.

And sometimes, legacy is born in the decisions, the shifts, and the yeses. From one place to another, from roommates to marriage, from walking to the bus stop to driving to work with worship music filling the car, I couldn't wait to see what God would do next.

The car I drove off that corner lot years before had witnessed my journey. It carried me through seasons of scarcity and answered countless prayers. I remember lending it to a friend in need, sharing the blessing it had been. To me, that car was a provision meant to be shared, not hoarded. I thought about those moments as my husband drove it to trade it in.

Letting go of that car was bittersweet. Standing on the lot, looking at it one last time, I felt a mix of loss and pride. That car had seen me through so much, but I knew its assignment in my life was over. It was time for someone else to be blessed as I had been.

This transition didn't feel like a loss; it felt like seed-sowing. By then, I wasn't just surviving anymore; I was planning. My husband had already purchased my next vehicle, a brand-new Saturn Aura, and he was trading in my old car to get himself a new one.

I had grown. I wasn't reacting to life anymore. I was responding with prayer, planning, and wisdom. Each step forward brought new clarity, deeper trust in God, and a firmer belief in myself. I was no longer just asking God to get me through the month; I was asking Him to help me build something that would last.

I knew, deep in my soul, that I had earned a seat at the table where faith is rewarded not because I had done everything perfectly, but because I had stayed the course. I had kept showing up. I tithed through ramen meals and praised through bus rides. I believed when the facts told me to quit. I dreamed when my surroundings gave me no reason to.

I had earned a seat prepared in faith, and now I was sitting on the promise. Holding that title in my hand for the last time, I thanked God for the opportunity to own that car.

I thanked Him for every mile I had walked, every tear I had cried, and every "not yet" that had turned into "right now." Because this seat, this moment, this life I was living was built on belief.

Chapter 13: Closed Doors and Quiet Fears

Sometimes, rejection isn't a red light; it's a reroute, pointing you toward something greater.

There's something profoundly humbling about starting at the bottom, even when you're holding a degree in your hand and dreams in your heart.

When I accepted my first job at the county office, I knew it wasn't my final destination. Still, I treated it like it mattered because it did. It was where I would learn how the system worked, how people were served, and how policies were applied in real time.

So, I got to work. I didn't just want to do the job; I wanted to understand it. I studied the manuals, learned the procedures, memorized the forms, and observed how the seasoned employees handled complex situations. If someone had a question, I wanted to be the one with the answer.

But I didn't stop there. Once I had mastered my own responsibilities, I began watching what was happening in other departments. I paid attention during staff meetings, asked questions during lunch breaks, and listened closely whenever leadership spoke. I wasn't trying to impress anyone; I was building a foundation. I was laying bricks with intention, knowing the day would come when I'd be ready to climb higher.

The next position in my department came with what I considered a significant pay increase, and yes, that alone was motivation. But more than that, it offered influence. It meant having a bigger voice in how we served people. I made a promise to myself then: I would never settle for where I was. I would always look for the next step on my terms, not anyone else's. That mindset became a compass for my entire career, guiding me in the good seasons and keeping me steady in the deeply disappointing ones.

Eventually, I earned a promotion within the county office. When I got the news, I didn't jump up and down or throw a party. I smiled, whispered a thank you to God, and got right back to work. For me, celebration came in the doing. This new position demanded just as much commitment as my first, if not more.

I studied that role with the same intensity I had brought to my first job. I didn't just want to meet expectations; I wanted to exceed them. I believed that if I kept growing, kept showing up and doing the work, even when no one was watching, I would be ready for the next opportunity when it came.

After a few years, I set my sights higher. I wanted to work at the state agency. That's where policies were shaped and decisions were made, decisions that directly impacted how frontline staff like me did our jobs. I wasn't chasing a title. I was seeking a seat at the table where change could truly happen.

So I started applying. Application after application. Résumé after résumé. I tailored each one carefully to match the posting, highlighting my experience, my promotion, and my dedication. I prayed over every submission, believing the right door would open.

For over a year, the responses were the same polite rejection letters thanking me for my interest and informing me someone else had been selected.

By then, applying had become almost a rhythm, a reflex. But it wasn't aimless. I only pursued roles that stirred something in me, jobs where my skills, passion, and purpose could meet. I didn't want to just clock in and out. I wanted to work on purpose. I wanted more than a paycheck. I wanted meaning.

With each application, I attached hope that the right door would open, that my "Yes" would come. Most of the time, I didn't get the response I wanted. Sometimes, there was no word at all, just silence stretching across days, then weeks. Other times, a brief email arrived, expressing appreciation for my interest.

At first, I brushed it off. "God's timing," I whispered. "What's for me is for me." And I believed it. I still do. But as the months turned into more months and the rejections piled higher than my confidence, the silence started to sound different. It wasn't just "No," it was "Not yet." And "Not yet" began to feel like "Never."

A slow voice crept into my thoughts, quiet but persistent, telling me I wasn't what they were looking for, that I wasn't as qualified as I thought, that I'd reached as far as I could go. I didn't stop applying. I didn't stop showing up. But I started shrinking not in my work ethic, but in my belief. The fire was still there, but it flickered intermittently. I'd show up with a smile, do my job, and feel unseen. How would it feel to be chosen? To have someone look at my résumé and want to hire me?

Meanwhile, I watched others move ahead of people with less experience, fewer credentials, some who had just arrived already soaring. I told myself not to compare. Comparison doesn't wait for an invitation. It shows up unannounced and sits quietly beside you in the breakroom while others talk about promotions and new opportunities.

It hurt. Not because I wasn't happy for them, I wanted that feeling too. That season taught me how to keep working with hope in my hands and disappointment in my heart. It taught me how to press forward when doors don't open and how to believe that God's "Yes" is still on the way, despite the responses I was getting.

I kept praying, pressing, and preparing. Even when rejection stung, I reminded myself that delay is not denial. Closed doors aren't always punishment; they're protection. Somewhere deep down, I still believed the right door wouldn't just open; it would swing wide with my name on it.

Still, I questioned whether my dreams were too big. Whether my faith was misplaced. Whether my story had already peaked, and I just hadn't realized it yet.
In the middle of those doubts, a small, still voice in my spirit kept whispering: Keep going. Keep applying. Keep trusting. You are not being overlooked; you are being positioned. That truth began to shift how I saw every rejection.

What I had once taken as a personal blow, every "thank you for your application" email that led to nowhere, was just a one-sided view. A paper version of me that a stranger glanced at for only a few minutes. They hadn't met me, heard my voice, felt my passion, or seen the years of perseverance I could never fully capture in a résumé or cover letter. They didn't know my story, and truthfully, I didn't know theirs.

I didn't know what went into their hiring process, what decisions had already been made, what constraints they were facing, or which other candidates they were considering. Yet every time that generic email hit my inbox, I let it speak to my worth. I let an electronic notification try to define me, if only for a moment.

It was a brutal cycle I had to unlearn. I realized I was seeing myself through the eyes of people who didn't really know me. I was letting their silence shout louder than God's still, small voice. His voice reminded me that my value didn't fluctuate with hiring cycles. My purpose wasn't waiting in someone's inbox for validation. A rejection didn't mean I wasn't enough. Sometimes, it simply meant the fit wasn't right or the season wasn't now.

That voice reminded me that God's plan didn't run on HR timelines. He wasn't just preparing a position. He was preparing me to fill it, molding me in the waiting, shaping me with humility, patience, and deeper wisdom. And when the right door finally opened, it wouldn't just be a job. It would be an assignment.

So, I kept pressing forward. I didn't stop learning. I didn't stop growing. I didn't stop applying not just to positions, but to the belief that I was called, qualified, and capable.

I no longer let rejection emails have the final word. They were data points, not destiny.

I kept praying, refining my skills, and envisioning the table I longed to sit at not as a dream, but as a destination designed just for me. Because even when you feel passed over, heaven has not forgotten your name. And when it's truly time, no closed door can keep you from the calling God has already prepared.

When the door finally opened and when that "yes" came, it wasn't just about the job. It was about every quiet moment that led to it: every prayer whispered while typing another application, every sigh released after another rejection, every "I'll try again" spoken into the silence.

I didn't know it then, but every closed door was a redirect not away from purpose, but toward it. I didn't know it then, but every closed door was a redirect not away from purpose, but toward it.

And when I finally walked through the right door, I carried more than a resume; I brought a history. A history of faithfulness, integrity, and the quiet, stubborn refusal to give up. And in that, I found peace.

Chapter 14: A Door Reopened

Eventually, the waiting ended. Not with a flash of lightning or a dramatic twist of fate, but on an ordinary, quiet day. I was at work, moving through routine tasks, my heart steady but tired. Hope had become a quiet companion—there, but silent. I'd learned not to expect too much. Disappointment taught me to soften my dreams, not clutch them too tightly.

After all the waiting, praying, applying, and nearly giving up, the phone finally rang. I answered, expecting a routine work call. A colleague. A reminder. Or maybe a robocall I'd ignore. But it wasn't. It was a voice I didn't recognize, asking to confirm my availability for an interview at the state office.

The very place I'd set my heart on. The office that had sent me countless "thank you for applying" emails. The office that had never even invited me inside.

Now, here they were asking me to come. Not because I begged. Not because someone pulled strings. But because something on paper made them decide to give me a chance. I jotted down the time and date with shaking hands. I thanked them. When the call ended, I sat in silence. No shouting. No tears. Just stillness. That moment carried weight.

I'd prayed for this not once, but consistently. I had spoken it aloud, dared to envision it, and now the door once sealed was cracking open. It wasn't just a job interview. It was a moment of hope a whisper saying, now is the time. Excitement and fear clashed in my chest like old rivals. I'd longed for this moment, but now that it was here, I feared mishandling it. So, I got to work.

I read the job description as if my future depended on it. Line by line, word by word, trying to understand precisely what they wanted and how I fit. I rehearsed potential questions and practiced aloud to avoid stumbling. I reflected on every project, every leadership moment, and every lesson learned from mistakes.

I went to my closet and chose my best outfit. Not flashy, just polished. I wanted to walk into that room looking like I belonged because I did. On the morning of the interview, I rose before the sun. I didn't turn on the music. I didn't rush. I sat quietly, Bible nearby, and prayed. "God, let me be fully me. Let me walk in peace. Let me speak clearly. And let whatever happens today bring me closer to where You want me."

Arriving at the state office, I felt small and large all at once. The lobby stretched wide, with gleaming floors, high ceilings, and glass doors opening and closing as professionals moved through. I didn't feel like an outsider. I didn't feel like an impostor. I felt expected. Like all those mornings walking to the bus stop. All those days whispering in my apartment, "God, let more be possible." All those applications that led nowhere. All of it had prepared me for this moment.

I checked in, took a seat, and looked around. The room buzzed with energy, but I remained still. I sat just past the halfway point, not in the back, not in the front. I didn't want to hide, but I also didn't want to stand out. That middle seat felt like a place to balance and ground myself.

Then, my name was called.

The panel interview felt both like a test and a testimony. Their questions were direct; their expressions unreadable. But I answered each quietly, with the confidence that comes from living the work. I didn't embellish. I didn't shrink. I spoke honestly and calmly, drawing from real experience, not theory.

I knew the program well. I'd seen it up close. I'd guided people through its requirements, answered tough questions, and navigated the complexities behind public service. I'd learned the policies, managed caseloads, and mentored others along the way. This wasn't a role I sought without a foundation. I'd grown into it step by step.

When the interview ended, I stood, thanked them sincerely, and walked out head held high. I didn't know if I'd get the job. I didn't know what would come next. But I knew I had shown up fully, faithfully, authentically. I didn't walk away certain, but I walked away peaceful knowing I had a chance. I allowed myself to hope.

I waited expectantly for the call, the one I was sure would change everything. Day after day, I checked my phone countless times. I re-read the job description, revisited their questions, and replayed the interview in my mind. I imagined the joy of hearing, "We'd like to offer you the position."

But instead, a letter arrived, and another candidate was chosen. The words didn't just sting, they hollowed me out. I blinked at the paper, willing the words to change. I had prayed, prepared, believed. All I had was another "no."

This time felt different. I thought I'd finally done enough, been enough, become enough. This wasn't just rejection. This was rejection after hope, the kind that hurts the most. That's the kind of disappointment that lingers. It doesn't scream; it whispers. It murmurs in quiet moments, planting doubt and fear. It doesn't just challenge your qualifications; it challenges your worth.

Maybe I was too confident. Perhaps I wasn't what they were looking for. Maybe I was foolish to believe it could happen.

Then came the questions deeper than credentials. Maybe I wasn't as capable as I thought. Perhaps I'd overestimated my purpose. Maybe I should stop hoping.

For days, the rejection felt like an invisible weight. It sat with me at my desk. It followed me home. It curled beside me at night like a shadow that wouldn't leave. I still showed up. I still smiled. But inside, I was unraveling not loudly, but slowly.

I drafted a message to the hiring manager, asking for feedback. If I knew what went wrong, maybe I could fix it. But I never sent it. Fear stopped me, fear of hearing something that confirmed my deepest insecurities. What if they said I wasn't a good fit? What if they said I didn't present well? Or that I lacked leadership presence? What if I'd reached the limit of what I was capable of?

So, I hit delete, but in the silence, God met me. He didn't rebuke me. He didn't rush me. He reminded me of something I had momentarily forgotten. He reminded me that what I saw as rejection didn't diminish my worth. It's not always a "no" to your calling. Sometimes, it's just not yet the right path. That letter didn't define me or erase all the preparation behind me. That silence didn't mean God had stopped speaking.

So, I got up again. I kept going because I had decided long before this moment that my belief in God's plan wasn't tied to man's response. I had to grieve that "No." But I also had to trust a "Yes" was coming. Not just any yes, but the right one. Slowly, I began to rise again, not because I felt strong, but because I chose not to stop.

Doors close. Hearts break. Dreams delay. But if the calling is real, if the assignment is divine, your yes won't pass you by. It may take longer. It may come through unexpected paths. But it will come. And when it does, you'll realize every closed door, every quiet fear, every tear-stained night was never wasted. They were making room, building resilience. Stretching your capacity, teaching you how to stand in the place you prayed for with humility and strength.

Part III: When Faith Gets Loud

Bold Prayers, Bolder Steps

Faith doesn't always look the way we expect. Sometimes, it seems like walking to the bus stop with your last ounce of dignity. In this season, my faith became something I chose to live out, day by day. This part of the story holds pivotal moments, leaving, leaping, applying, surviving, and showing up anyway.

Chapter 15: Destiny

I felt rejected and needed to regroup. I wasn't giving up, but I needed a moment to catch my breath and process what had happened. The rejection was hard, but my resilience was growing. My resilience was quiet, waiting to rise again.

Then it happened. I was working when the phone rang. The caller asked if I wanted to interview at the state office. This interview was for a different department than my previous one. This time felt different. Not because the job was easier or the circumstances had miraculously improved. No, it was different because I was different.

I had walked through the fire of disappointment and emerged wiser, tougher, and surer of who I was.

I was still expecting. I stayed faithful, even when it hurt. I showed up when I wanted to shrink back. I trusted God when it would have been easier to stop believing. I'd done the work inside and out.

Now, a small ember of hope burned steadily in my chest. Something was turning. Something was about to break open.

I accepted the interview without hesitation. I pulled out my notebook, studied the posting, reviewed my experiences, and rehearsed my strengths. This time, I prepared with less fear and more clarity. I now knew rejection wasn't a verdict on my worth, it was a redirection. I'd already proven to myself I could survive a "no." I'd already survived worse.

Still, nothing prepared me for what happened when I arrived. As I stepped through the familiar glass doors, my heart sank into my stomach. It was the same department as my last interview.

The same waiting area, neutral-colored chairs, muted artwork. The same carpet I had nervously crossed months before. The same knot of anxiety formed in my gut as memories of the previous interview and painful rejection flooded back. I felt paralyzed.
What if someone from the previous hiring panel saw me? What if the manager who had chosen someone else walked by and recognized me? I could already see the pity in their eyes, the quiet judgment, the whispered questions: Why is she back? Didn't she get the message the first time?

I sat in the chair, painfully visible yet desperate to disappear. I wanted to hide in plain sight to melt into the beige walls, to shrink into invisibility until called.

I forced myself to steady my breathing in, out, in, out.

I whispered silent prayers, clutching my bag strap like an anchor. I reminded myself of every truth I'd fought so hard to believe. Truths like: I am not a mistake. I am not unworthy. I reminded myself I am here on purpose.

Still, my fear was real. I felt small, exposed, vulnerable. I also felt something else, something rooted deep inside me through every closed door and lonely bus stop walk.

I felt resolved. I'd come too far to let fear win now. I'd sacrificed too much to bow to shame. I wasn't sitting there by accident. I was sitting there by divine appointment. God had allowed me to return to the place of my rejection. This wasn't to humiliate me; it was to elevate me beyond my perceived circumstances.

This wasn't just another interview. It was a test of endurance. Sitting there, holding my notes and smoothing my skirt, I decided that whatever happened next, I wouldn't shrink back. I would show up fully, boldly, authentically because no matter who recognized me, God saw me and wasn't finished with my story. Not by a long shot.

Eventually, the hiring manager came from the other side of the department and greeted me warmly. The interview began. Like before, it was a panel setting. Questions came, and I answered with honesty, confidence, and grace. This time, I relaxed and engaged with the interviewers as if I belonged there.

I left feeling at peace. I had shown up as the fullest version of myself. Weeks later, the call came, and I got the job. I nearly dropped the phone. I had to sit down. Tears blurred my vision as I steadied my voice to say, "Thank you." This wasn't just a job offer. It was redemption. Validation. Physical proof of every prayer, every private war, every ounce of obedience to keep going when everything inside me said, "Give up."

The first days on the job felt like a dream. I made it.
I went from a county caseworker in a small cubicle to a state agency, where policies take shape, and I was seen as a leader. The ladder I once stared up at, wondering if it was built for people like me, I was now climbing steadily, with strong hands and a strong heart.

Throughout my preparation, one lingering fear followed me. It followed me in quiet moments. It crept up while I ironed my clothes for work. It whispered when I reread the welcome packet and imagined my new office.

What would happen if the hiring manager, the one who didn't choose me, saw me there? What would she think? Would she run to my new supervisor and whisper doubts? Would she try to undermine me before I had a chance to prove myself? Would she see me walking those halls and shake her head, thinking I didn't belong?

I was terrified of being seen and misunderstood. Even though I had prayed, believed, and prepared, the weight of those unspoken questions pressed against my ribs. I scanned the waiting area every time I walked through it.

My heart raced at every familiar face. I didn't want to be caught off guard. I was bracing myself for a blow that might never come. It didn't steal my happiness about the job, but it muted it. I celebrated quietly. I smiled outwardly. But inside, part of me held its breath.

I wanted to be fully at peace. I wanted to move forward without fear. Sometimes peace takes time to catch up with your feet, even when your spirit knows you're precisely where you should be.

Then it happened.

One afternoon, as I warmed up my lunch, I heard someone call my name across the room. I froze. I turned slowly and there she was.

The hiring manager from the previous interview. The woman whose imagined rejection had haunted me for months. The one I thought had dismissed me. The one I feared had seen me and decided I wasn't good enough. She walked toward me, smiling. Genuinely.

My heart raced not from fear, but from stunned disbelief. With genuine warmth, she said, "Donna! I didn't know you were here! You should have told me you were one of the best interviews we had. I wanted to recommend you, but the decision was made to hire someone internally."

I stood there, stunned into silence. Every fearful thought. Every sleepless night. Every moment of self-doubt—all undone in a single moment of unexpected kindness. She hadn't dismissed me; she valued me. I had carried the weight of a lie.

I believed her silence meant disapproval and her choice meant condemnation, but it hadn't. God had been protecting the timing, not punishing my efforts. The no wasn't because I wasn't enough. It was simply because it wasn't the right door at that time. And now, here I stood not hidden or ashamed, but welcomed.

In that moment, I realized I'd been holding my breath for a long time, and I could finally exhale. The tension I'd carried, the fear of being overlooked, misunderstood, or rejected, loosened its grip.

I realized I never needed to hide. I never needed to apologize for being where God placed me. I was seen and valued. I was exactly where I was meant to be.

It wasn't man's approval that sealed it; it was God's hand weaving affirmation into an ordinary afternoon, proving once again that His timing is perfect, His promises sure, and His love always finds us, even in unexpected places.

In that moment, a lesson took root in me one I'd carry for life: Never let someone else's silence become your story. What you assume is a no because of who you are has nothing to do with your worth. Sometimes, the answer is no because someone else needed their turn. The door wasn't yours.

I thanked her not just for the kind words, but for the confirmation I hadn't even realized I needed. I walked back to my desk with peace, confidence, and renewed resolve.

This new position brought new challenges, of course. I was now working on systems that supported frontline workers. It was less client-facing and more technical. But the mission hadn't changed. I was still serving people, just in a different capacity. I brought the same heart, the same dedication, and the same "I want to learn everything" mindset that had carried me through every role.

Truthfully, what is yours won't miss you. It might be delayed. You may have to detour. It may come through tears, silence, and a great deal of waiting. But if it belongs to you, it will come, and when it does, you won't have to beg for it. You won't have to manipulate it.

You'll walk into it with the kind of peace that only comes from knowing this is God's doing.

Chapter 16: When the Ground Shakes

By the time I settled into my new role at the state office, it felt like I had finally arrived at a place of peace. Not perfection, just peace. The grind to get there, the countless rejections, moments of self-doubt, quiet waiting, and years of piecing together faith and food had softened into a rhythm. I knew my responsibilities. My coworkers were kind. And for the first time in a long while, we could breathe financially.

I had been working for the state for less than nine years, but had grown into the space. It didn't take long to master the work. I could do it with my eyes closed. Though I knew deep down I was created for face-to-face impact, speaking, teaching, and direct connection, the warmth and safety of that environment made it easy to settle in. It felt like family. We checked on each other, shared laughs over lunch, offered prayers during challenges, and celebrated personal milestones together. In a harsh world, this was sacred ground.

I decided not to look beyond my area when thinking about my future. Movement, if any, would be internal. I was content with how things were and where I was. I had endured to get there, and this comfort felt like a gift.

My days were spent behind the scenes managing systems, analyzing data, and resolving issues others might overlook. It wasn't always glamorous, but I understood its value. To some, it seemed boring or overly technical. To me, it was an opportunity to build, streamline, and serve, making others' jobs easier and more efficient.

Though I wouldn't have called myself a tech person, I had a gift for the job. I could see patterns. I could follow the thread of a problem from surface to source. I didn't just react, I could anticipate. I knew when something on the front end didn't look quite right. The issue was usually buried deeper, waiting to be addressed. That instinct made me a go-to person when things went wrong, and I didn't take that lightly. It gave me purpose. Even though I wasn't face-to-face with the people we served, I knew I was still helping from another angle.

It was quiet, fulfilling work, and I planned to stay until I retired. I could picture myself in that office for the long haul. The peace was good, too rare to let go easily. Comfort, I'd learned, doesn't always mean permanence. Peace doesn't always mean the assignment is complete.

In 2003, the agency announced a Reduction-in-Force (RIF). It wasn't the first time I'd heard those words, but this time something felt different, more real. I had been a government employee for less than ten years. I had a chance to avoid being RIFed. The agency was allowing exceptions; unfortunately, no one asked for one on my behalf. When the list came out, I was the eighth person let go.

Seniority often decided who stayed and who didn't. No matter how much I contributed, the numbers weren't in my favor. The only positive was the chance of being recalled within the next year if the agency rehired for my position title. The irony wasn't lost on me. I worked in systems designed to provide stability, yet now I faced instability.

Even though I could do the job with ease, even though I loved my team and felt deeply rooted in that space, I sensed the winds shifting. My spirit began to stir. I didn't want to leave, but I had learned that when God shifts the atmosphere, it's not about comfort, it's about calling.

Still, when the formal notice arrived, it hit me like a punch to the stomach. The job that once felt like a safe landing was now the start of another climb. Another transition. Another test of faith. But this time, I wasn't the same woman who had stood in borrowed clothes and caught buses in the rain. I didn't know what lay ahead. I knew peace wasn't just found in a workplace. Peace followed me because the One who gave it still walked with me.

To make matters harder, I had a two-year-old at home and a household depending on my income. There's a particular kind of weight you carry as a parent. It's not just about what you lose; it's about who depends on you to hold everything together while you're breaking apart.

When I think back to that season, I can't separate it from the memory of my pregnancy.

It was a high-risk pregnancy, and I felt every bit of that label. From the fifth month onward, I was in and out of the hospital, battling constant nausea and dehydration. I had hyperemesis gravidarum, a condition often mistaken for morning sickness but far more severe. I was losing weight when I should have been gaining.

I couldn't keep food or water down. My body felt like it was betraying me, but I pushed through because there was life growing inside me, a life I had prayed for.

At one point, I was pregnant with twins. I remember looking at that ultrasound, heart full of wonder, feeling like God was multiplying joy after such a long season of endurance. Twins hadn't skipped a generation in my family for at least three generations. My dad had twin siblings, and my mom had twins;

Here I was, fulfilling a family legacy. Months later, during a follow-up appointment, I lay on the table again and heard words that made my heart sink. The doctor could find only one heartbeat. Only one baby was visible. One of the twins had vanished, they explained, absorbed. It was called vanishing twin syndrome. Though I still had a healthy baby inside me, I felt the loss like a vacuum in my womb. I felt joy and grief side by side.

Still, I kept working. I kept showing up. Even when physically weak, even when my body trembled from exhaustion, I showed up.

I remember the day my supervisor visited me in the hospital, IVs in my arm, monitors beeping in the background. She walked in holding an evaluation form. Not to pressure me, but to advocate on my behalf. To ensure that, even amid uncertainty about my condition and rumors of an impending Reduction-in-Force (RIF), my value was recognized and remembered. She didn't have to do that, but she did. That moment reminded me that even within bureaucracies and impersonal systems, humanity can still show up. I was more than a name on a payroll list. I was someone worth fighting for.

I had lost a job, but I had not lost my calling. I had lost an income, but I had not lost myself. Even my supervisor's efforts, though deeply appreciated, couldn't stop what was coming. The agency delayed the inevitable as long as they could. There were talks. Attempts to restructure. They did everything they could to keep positions. I clung to it with all the faith I could muster. I wanted to believe my job was safe. Then the letter came: I was Riffed.

Just like that, the life I had built my stability on cracked. The job that had been a hard-earned victory was now gone. I was officially jobless, burdened with questions too heavy to voice. It wasn't just about income; it was about identity, security, and losing the routine and rhythm I had fought so hard to build. We were already living paycheck to paycheck, carefully budgeting groceries and gas. What were we going to do now? Where would we go from here?

There's a unique kind of grief that sets in when something stable is taken not violently, not all at once, but quietly, like a door closing slowly behind you. I had shown up. I had done the work. I took the bus. Climbed the ladder. Proved myself time and again.

And still, I was left feeling empty. As I sat in the uncertainty, something more profound began to rise in me.

Amid my grief, I did something unexpected. I sat down and wrote an email not to plead for my job back, but to encourage the very woman who had to make the difficult decision to let me go. Some might think it unwise, but for me, it was necessary. My peace didn't come from a paycheck; it came from knowing I had honored God, even in the most challenging moments.

Here is what I wrote:
Dear Director,
My name is Donna Davis, and I am one of the employees who lost her job due to the RIF. I am writing to acknowledge that you had to make difficult decisions for the efficiency of the agency. I served as a Program Coordinator I for over eight years, progressing through promotions from Economic Service Case Worker and Family Independence Case Worker roles.

My immediate concern was for my two-year-old son until I came to realize that my family belongs to God. I trust Him to provide for and care for us. I am writing to encourage you. I know you have been placed in a difficult position, but since you came to DSS, and I met you during the drop-in, I know you are a sincere person.

Honestly, I thought I would retire from DSS. I love what I do so much. I'm currently looking for a new job, but I have peace from God and trust that I will find something soon. I also care deeply about the progress of DSS. The Lord has given me peace through this experience.

I would like to share a scripture with you: Philippians 4:13 "For I know the plans I have for you," declares the Lord, "plans to prosper you and not to harm you, plans to give you hope and a future."

It has been a privilege working for you. God bless you.

I reflected on my track record of faithfulness: the candy bar moments, the fake steering wheel mornings, whispered prayers at the bus stop, and the promotions that followed prayer and perseverance. I reminded myself this was not the end, but another turn in the story.

There were days when I cried, when fear was so loud, I couldn't focus on anything else, but there were also days I pressed my hand to my heart and assured myself that things would be okay.

I learned that trust doesn't always roar. Sometimes, it sits quietly beside your uncertainty and whispers, "Even now, God sees this and He always has."

I believe God used every situation. The shake-up didn't destroy me; it positioned me. It woke something inside me that comfort had allowed to lie dormant. This loss wasn't a closed door at all. Maybe it was a hand reaching down, inviting me to rise higher.

I didn't know what was coming next, but I knew God wastes nothing. Not my pregnancy complications. Not my job loss. Not even the ache of unanswered prayers.

He was still writing, and the next chapter was already unfolding, even if I couldn't see it yet.

Chapter 17: A Letter of Peace

The Reduction in Force could have broken me, and in many ways, it tried. I had overcome so much to get where I was, pushing through rejection, disappointment, and uncertainty. I had finally found my rhythm in a role that challenged and fulfilled me, only to watch it slip right through my fingers.

There's something deeply unsettling about being let go not because of poor performance or any mistake of your own, but simply because the numbers no longer add up in your favor. It felt cold, impersonal, and unfair. Still, I knew that on the other side of that decision were real people forced to make impossible choices.

I didn't know the director of our agency. I'd seen her once or twice at events, maybe passed her in a hallway. But I could imagine the weight she carried, not just the pressure of cutting staff, but the emotional toll of telling people they no longer had a job. These were people with families, bills, responsibilities, just like me.

I could have kept my thoughts to myself, written them down in a journal, whispered them in prayer, and moved on. But something inside me stirred, compelling me to do something different.

I chose to write her an email. Not to accuse. Not to plead. But to speak peace. I sat at my computer and typed out what was on my heart, no bitterness, no blame, just the truth. My truth.

I told her my name. I told her I was one of those who were let go. I explained how I'd worked my way up through the ranks, starting from an entry-level role and moving with quiet diligence until I reached a position where I believed I could make a lasting difference. And I told her I understood.

I recognized the gravity of her role. I knew these decisions were never made lightly. Though the outcome grieved me, I held no resentment toward her. Then, I told her that I trusted God to care for me and my family. Even though my name was on the list, it was also written in the palm of God's hand. I shared the scripture that had carried me through so many storms:

"For I know the plans I have for you," declares the Lord. "Plans to prosper you, not to harm you. Plans to give you a future and a hope." (Jeremiah 29:11)

I told her I still believed in the agency's mission. Though my position was gone, my faith was not. I was telling her I was walking away with grace, not bitterness. I was walking away with dignity, not defeat. Then I hit send.

It may seem like just an email or words on a screen, but to me, it was a release. A way to tell God that I trusted Him, no matter the circumstances. A way of reminding myself that peace was still within my power to choose.

Sometimes we think strength only looks like standing firm and fighting back. And yes, there is power in protest, resistance, in raising your voice when needed. But strength also takes a softer form. It looks like choosing peace when pain would be easier. It seems like sending a blessing when you could have sent blame. Honoring the journey, even the parts that didn't go as planned, is essential.

That email wasn't just for the agency director; it was for me. It was my way of taking the high road without pretending the road hadn't hurt. It was my reminder that I could walk through loss with grace, and even when the world shifted beneath my feet, I didn't have to lose who I am.

I was. At that moment, I didn't know what would come next. I had no new job lined up. No guarantee of what tomorrow would bring. But I knew who I was, and that was enough.

When the world tells you it's over, but God says, I'm not done, that's when comebacks are born.

After being RIF'ed, I did what I had always done when life unraveled: I picked up the pieces and moved forward. This time, it didn't feel like starting over. It felt like I was starting from wisdom.

I wasn't the same woman who applied for jobs from a boarding house room or whispered prayers on a bus bench. I had grown through valleys, victories, and every act of obedience in between. This time, I had a history with God. A track record. Evidence that He had seen me through before.

Still, the process wasn't easy. Submitting applications became routine again. But my perspective had shifted since my last job. I wasn't searching for just any job; I was searching for alignment. Purpose. A new place to serve that wouldn't erase what I had lost but would honor what I still carried.

I targeted two familiar locations: my local county office and one in a neighboring county where I had worked my very first job.

Returning to those places wasn't a step backward; it was reclaiming. A declaration that just because life had taken an unexpected turn didn't mean I was off course. Soon after, I received a call from the local office in my county. They wanted to interview me.

I remember getting dressed for that interview, standing in front of the mirror longer than usual. I wasn't anxious about how I looked; I was worried about what I might feel. Would I break down talking about being laid off? Would they see the weariness before they saw my worth?

Walking into that building was surreal. So many memories surfaced from the early days of my career, the hunger I once had to prove I could do the work. Now, I wasn't trying to prove myself. I was showing up as who I had become.

The hiring manager greeted me with a warmth that instantly calmed my nerves. Her eyes lit up when she saw me, and in that moment, I knew I was welcomed.

My former supervisor had been advocating for me the entire time. She sent word ahead of me. Spoke my name with honor. Let others know that Donna Davis wasn't just dependable, she was a light, a force, a presence that made things better. That kind of advocacy can't be bought or strategized. It comes from showing up day after day with integrity and heart, even when no one's clapping.

As I sat across from the hiring manager, I didn't hold back. I told her the truth. I had been RIF'ed, and while there was a chance I might be recalled to the state office, I didn't know how or when that would happen. I wanted to be upfront. No surprises.

She paused, nodded, and then said the kind of words that reach deep into your soul. "Even if I only have you for a month," she said with conviction, "my department will be better because you were here." Those words made me blink back tears. That wasn't just a compliment. That was confirmation. That was God showing me that the work I'd done, the faith I'd lived, the love I'd poured into every hallway and hallway conversation had not gone unnoticed.

That moment healed something inside me. It reminded me that being laid off didn't mean I had lost my value. That detours don't destroy destiny. That's when the world says no, God still writes yes in places your feet haven't touched yet.

I left that interview feeling lighter than I had in months because I realized something powerful: rejection might redirect your path, but it can't remove your purpose. Despite being RIF'ed, I was still walking in mine.

However, my heart sank the moment I heard the salary offer. It wasn't just lower it was the bottom of the pay scale. I tried to stay composed, but inwardly, it felt like a gut punch. I had years of experience, a strong track record, and a résumé that showed results. I had walked through fire to get here, and now I was being asked to start again for over $10,000 less than what I'd been earning.

Still, I gathered my courage and asked for more. I reminded them gently but firmly of what I brought to the table. Of what I knew. Of what I had already proven. To their credit, they honored me with a 10% increase, but even then, the salary still sat far below what I had left behind.

It stung, but I had learned something in the valley seasons of my life. Provisions don't always come in whole paychecks. Sometimes, it comes through open doors. In assignments wrapped in obedience. In temporary places that prepare you for a permanent purpose. So, I said yes.

Between being RIF'ed from my role and starting fresh at Lexington County DSS, a quiet panic threatened to set in. We were going to miss a whole paycheck during the transition, and this wasn't a minor inconvenience. It was a significant disruption, a gap we couldn't afford. There were bills, groceries, needs, and no room for delay.

But God had already made a way. Not just days before, but five years earlier. When I bought my car five years ago, the financier offered an optional maintenance protection plan. I didn't want it. It felt like another upcharge, another add-on I couldn't afford to prioritize. Then he said something that made me pause.

He said if I didn't use the maintenance within five years, I could request a full refund. It wouldn't be automatic; I would have to ask for it, but I would receive it. Something about that statement stayed with me. Against all logic, I agreed and made a note literally. I marked the date on my digital calendar. I didn't know then that I was setting a divine appointment.

Five years later, the reminder popped up on my calendar. I remembered the plan. I filed the request, and I received the check. It was within $100 of the paycheck I had missed. Not hundreds of dollars short. Not strangely off. Just a few dollars different from what I would have earned had I never been RIF'ed at all.

We did not miss a beat. Our needs were met. I sat in awe, holding that check in my hands, not because it came from a dealership or a finance office, but because it came from a God who plans. A God who provides before you even know you'll need it. A God who gently nudges your hand on a paper, even when you don't understand why you're signing.

That refund wasn't just money, it was proof. Proof that God is in the margins. Proof that even when income stops, provision doesn't. Proof that what feels small, like marking a calendar, can become a lifeline in the valley. He provided before the crisis. He saw the gap before I ever walked into it. He remembered when I didn't even know I'd forget.

It reminded me that faith isn't just about trusting God in the fire. It's about trusting that He stocked the shelves before the storm.

For two months, I served at Lexington County DSS. I didn't walk in bitter or entitled. I walked in grateful. Ready. Present. The work reminded me of why I started in the first place. I was back on the frontlines, face to face with people, meeting fundamental needs, making eye contact with those holding on by a thread. It was humbling. It was holy. It was healing.

I brought my whole heart to every task. Even though I knew this might not be my permanent stop, I treated it as if it were. Every client. Every application. Every moment of dignity I offered someone else mattered.

One day, a certified letter arrived. I held it in my hands as if it were fragile. My fingers trembled as I opened the envelope, my heart thudding with a mix of hope and fear, wrapped in equal measure. The letter informed me I was being recalled to the state agency. It wasn't the same office I had left. It wasn't the same team I had built a community with. But it was a way back to the state agency.

I showed up to meet the hiring manager, cautiously optimistic, and her reception was not exactly welcoming.

She wasn't unkind, nor was she excited. I could feel stiffness and unspoken questions. She was direct and honest, telling me she had hoped to hire someone of her choosing, someone she had selected, someone she had a hand in vetting.

I didn't take it personally. I understood. The rule was clear: positions eliminated through a Reduction in Force had to be offered first to the top eligible candidates on the recall list. I was number eight. The seven before me had either declined the offer or held a different title.
So here I was, not chosen but positioned. And there's a difference.

People can overlook you, and you can still be handpicked for a purpose. I nodded as she spoke. I offered my gratitude with humility. In my heart, I made a decision right there at her desk: I will not let this be a setback. I will let it be a setup.

I didn't walk into that department with resentment. I walked in with quiet determination. I wasn't there to convince anyone I belonged, I was there to show it. I knew my character. I knew my capacity. I knew my calling.

So, I leaned into the unfamiliar. I asked questions. I paid attention. I studied. I listened twice as much as I spoke.

I didn't demand respect; I earned it, day by day, word by word, task by task. While the welcome might not have been warm, I knew God had let me back in for a reason. This wasn't the end of the story. This was the middle of a miracle. From that day forward, I showed up with everything I had to offer.

I silenced every voice of doubt that tried to follow me through the door and made a quiet vow to let my work speak for me. So I did the work. I asked questions. I stayed late when needed and showed up early, not to impress, but to honor the opportunity I had been given. I learned the systems, adapted to unfamiliar routines, and found ways to make things easier for the team, all while continuing to get to know myself. I looked for ways to be helpful, then stepped in without waiting to be asked. Little by little, I saw a shift.

The same supervisor who once sat across from me with a calm demeanor began to warm up. Her posture softened. Her trust grew. Though she never said it directly at first, I could see the difference in how she began to include me in conversations, ask for my insight, and start to count on me.

Her walls began to lower not because I forced them, but because I built a bridge of consistency and care. My values spoke louder than my title. I didn't walk around boasting about what I had done or where I had been. I just let my faithfulness speak. And over time, it spoke loudly.

Then, one day, the very supervisor who had once given me that heartfelt recommendation to Lexington County DSS, the one who had believed in me when I wasn't sure I could believe in myself, reached out. She wanted to bring me back to her area. She asked if I'd consider returning to her department to work for her again. Something surprising happened as I considered the offer: my current supervisor didn't want to let me go.

The one who initially hadn't chosen me, who had been unsure about my fit, now didn't want to lose me. She had come to rely on my presence, my work ethic, and my spirit. What had started as an obligation had become a connection. I wasn't just a name on a recall list; I had become a part of her team.

That moment was deeply affirming. It wasn't about praise. It wasn't about power. It was about purpose. It was evidence that when you bring your whole self to the table, whether you're invited or placed, God will honor it.

Eventually, I returned to the department I had left before the RIF. I came back with more confidence, resilience, and clarity. I carried a testimony in my spirit that even detours are part of destiny. Those two months in Lexington County weren't a loss. It wasn't a fallback. It was a bridge. A refining. A proving ground. A reintroduction to myself.

It reminded me that God doesn't just restore what you lost. He rebuilds it better. Stronger. Wiser. With a depth that only the valley can teach. Restoration isn't about returning to where you were. Restoration is about walking into where you're meant to be with the strength of where you've been folded into every step.

I was ready for whatever came next.

Chapter 19: The Gut Punch

By 2005, something inside me began to stir. I had grown comfortable in my role, not in a lazy or unmotivated way, but in the kind of way that makes you realize you've mastered the terrain and are no longer being stretched. I knew my job inside and out.

I executed tasks with ease, led department meetings confidently, represented our team at agency-wide discussions, and mentored those who came after me. My name was known. My work was trusted. I believed my presence had value.

Comfort has a subtle way of becoming confinement when your soul is craving expansion. I started dreaming of more. More impact. More responsibility. More growth. Not because I was discontent, but because I could feel the capacity inside me pressing against the walls of where I was. It wasn't about chasing a title or trying to prove something; it was about purpose. I felt God nudging me, telling me I had served well and that now it was time to stretch my abilities. So, when I saw the job posting at another state agency, I paused for a moment.

The description read like it had been pulled straight from my résumé. It was work I was already doing without the formal title. I knew I was capable of doing the job. I knew I could make a difference. And just as important, I knew I was ready.

There was nothing frantic about my application. I didn't apply because I was desperate to escape. I applied because it felt like a door opening, and I had learned to trust open doors. Out of respect and professionalism, I sat down with my supervisor to let her know the agency and position I had applied for. I didn't want her blindsided by a reference request or an exit notice if I got the job.

I wanted her to hear it from me. She had been good to me. She supported my growth, advocated for me, and trusted me with leadership responsibilities. Our relationship was cordial and collaborative.
That conversation changed everything.

Days later, my supervisor came into my office wearing a look I couldn't quite read. She told me she had looked up the position I applied for and decided to apply for it herself. It took a moment for her words to register. I smiled tightly and nodded, but inside, I was spinning.

Wait, what? I thought. You applied for the same job? I was stunned, not angry, just caught off guard. I hadn't even considered withholding the information from her. I had shared my plans in good faith. I had opened the door to transparency and walked through it. Was it her right? Absolutely. But that didn't make it hurt any less.

We both received first-round interviews, followed by second-round interviews. Then the outcome came.
She got the job.

I was devastated. I didn't cry at my desk. I didn't storm out. I didn't throw a fit. I did what I had always done: I showed up. I smiled. I hosted her going-away celebration. I coordinated the decorations, gathered signatures for the farewell card, and made sure the refreshments were just right. Standing at the front of the room, I gave a speech wishing her well.

Still, I tried to comfort myself. This meant her position would become available. I would finally step into the seat I'd been prepared for all along. I allowed myself to believe that I was surely the natural successor.

I had done the work. I had shown loyalty. I had built systems, led projects, mentored team members, and held that department together during challenging transitions. I had proven my ability.

However, as I would soon learn, what is evident to you is not always apparent to others. What feels like betrayal can sometimes be preparation.

When people disappoint us, God is not confused. When the door we thought was ours swings shut, heaven is still at work behind the scenes. This wasn't just a gut punch; it was a test of character. Even though it bruised my spirit, it wouldn't break my purpose. I didn't know it at the time, but what felt like the most significant setback was about to push me toward one of the most important seasons of my life.

Sometimes, you don't realize you're in a launching season until your heart hits the ground. Here's what I've come to understand: You can honor someone and still feel the pain. You can celebrate them and still grieve your loss. And you can survive a gut punch and come out stronger than ever.

Chapter 20: When They Choose Someone Else

There's a unique pain in being passed over for something you've already proven you can do. Yet, there is also power in how you choose to rise from it.

After competing with my supervisor for a position, I kept working, not because I had figured out how to process it all; truthfully, I hadn't. I was still stunned and emotionally winded, but life doesn't wait for your healing to catch up. Of course, the employer chose the most experienced person for the job. I was left wondering if she would have applied if I hadn't mentioned it.

I moved as if carrying an invisible weight, not angry, not bitter, just trying to find my footing again. I had no energy for protest or resentment. So, I let peace find me through purpose. When her position became vacant, I didn't wait for an invitation; I stepped up and filled the gap. No announcements. No raised hand. Just presence.

I stepped in and kept the department steady. It wasn't performative or for show; it was simply who I was. I cared about the work and the people. I knew how critical it was for my department to stay afloat during the leadership transition. So, I led meetings, managed projects, answered emails that were once hers, and sat in meetings she used to attend, all with reverence, not for the title, but for the trust placed in me.

Without the authority of the title, I carried it in my posture. But I was careful not to assume that stepping in meant entitlement to stay. I respected the chain of command and knew how easy it was to be overlooked when leadership's attention was pulled in a million directions. I did something wise and vulnerable: I kept the director informed.

I updated her weekly to steward the opportunity, ensure alignment, and lead as she expected. When the position was officially posted, I applied not out of desperation or pride, but with calm confidence. Not entitlement, but clarity.

I had already been doing the job and had proven myself in practice. The department was thriving not because of a grand gesture, but because I held it together with strength and consistency. I knew the culture, the challenges, and I had built trust. The transition hadn't been confusing because I had stepped up.

On the day of my interview, I walked in with a sense of peace. But that peace began to shift the moment the interview started. The conversation felt more casual than professional, and job duties were barely mentioned.

There was an air of finality in the room, but not the kind that made you feel chosen. It felt like a conversation for the sake of appearance, casual, surface-level. Then came a moment I'll never forget. The hiring authority smiled gently and mentioned my faith.

She said something like, "Well, we know the power of God in our lives," nodding in that familiar, polite way that felt more like a benediction than a confirmation. It felt like a soft letdown wrapped in spiritual language.

I left her office confused. My head was spinning not from nerves, but from knowing, from sensing what wasn't being said. My heart, still tender from the last disappointment, was trying to shield itself from another. Yet, even as I walked to my car, I couldn't stop dreaming.

I began formulating plans in my mind about how I'd lead the department, strengthen systems, and bring fresh vision to the role. My heart had already said yes, even though my ears hadn't heard a word.

Later, my director called me into her office. She wanted to tell me in person that I hadn't gotten the job; she didn't want to send the news by email. The person selected was a relative of my former supervisor.

I stood there in silence, disbelief washing over me. The hope, labor, and leadership I'd modeled seemed dismissed. Holding my breath, steadying my voice, I let it settle over me like a storm cloud. The expectation was clear: accept and support the decision. Smile through it. Help facilitate it. And I did. But not before I spoke my truth.

I spoke firmly, not furiously. I didn't raise my voice or cry. I told her I was deeply disappointed. That I'd given my heart to this work, that I had trusted those in charge, only to now help someone else do the job I was already doing. Then I shared what was really in my spirit. I told her that if I weren't a mother with a child depending on me, I would have walked out that day. That's how hurt I was.

She barely blinked. With a shrug and a dismissive sigh, she said, "Donna, that happens every day."
My spirit recoiled. I retorted, "Happens to who?" I stared at her, silent words failing me, but her response spoke volumes. She had made peace with her decision.

I walked out of that office, and something shifted inside me. Not anger, but something more profound. Something truer. It was resolve. A revelation.

That was the moment I decided I would never again be caught off guard. I would never wait passively for someone to validate what God had already affirmed in me. I didn't storm out or get petty. Instead, I returned to my desk and did the job with dignity. I helped my new supervisor with the same care and clarity I would have offered anyone. My integrity wasn't for sale, and I refused to let decisions beyond my control make me bitter.

Yet, while assisting, I was like a builder. While explaining systems, I was strategizing. While handing over binders and login instructions, I prayed God would lead me to a place where I could serve in silence and flourish.

Yes, I was hurting. But I wasn't hopeless.

I was awake. Somehow, I didn't fall apart. By now, I had learned my value isn't defined by who chooses me. My calling isn't canceled because someone else was selected. God doesn't forget. Every seed planted. Every sacrifice made. Every silent act of faithfulness counts.

Even though this hurt, I knew one thing that couldn't be shaken: what is mine cannot be taken. It may be delayed. It may be detoured. But it cannot be denied.

So, I held my head high. I kept doing the work. I continued to serve the people and trusted the One who had never failed me yet. This wasn't the end of my story. It was just another chapter in the making of something greater.

I started reading more, learning more, asking questions, and observing how decisions were made, not just on paper, but in spirit. I stopped waiting for open doors and began preparing to build them.

This is for the person reading who relates to this: if you've ever trained someone less qualified, if you've ever watched a door, you were ready for it to swing open for someone else, if you've ever felt your heart break in silence while clapping for another's win, please know you are not overlooked. You are being cultivated. You are not stuck. You are being positioned.

The fire you feel is not bitterness, it's brilliance. Let it warm you, not consume you. What they didn't see, what they couldn't steal, was the purpose God planted in you.
Purpose doesn't need permission. Purpose doesn't need applause. Purpose doesn't even need fairness. It just requires faith.

So, I stayed, but I didn't settle. I served, but I also studied. I obeyed, but I also dreamed.

And one day, when the next opportunity arrives, when the door opens not because someone vouched for me, but because I was called, I'll be ready.

I'm not just showing up anymore. I'm sowing. And sowing always leads to harvest.

Even if the field looks unfair. Even if the reapers arrive late. Even if those in power don't believe in your roots.

The harvest still comes. And when it does, no one will be able to say you didn't earn it because while they watched, you grew.

Part IV: Delayed Does Not Mean Denied

Grace in the Waiting

Waiting seasons don't mean nothing is happening. These years taught me the strength of staying faithful when everything in me wanted to give up. Some doors didn't open to promotions that others received, and I learned to work with excellence in the shadows. What looked like a delay was divine preparation.

When the time was right, purpose called me forward not as the woman who had been passed over, but as the woman who had been prepared.

Chapter 21: Out of the Shadow

By 2006, I had lived long enough to recognize when a moment was more than just another open door; it was a divine pivot. I had walked through seasons of disappointment so layered they nearly clouded my ability to hope. I had carried the weight of being overlooked and passed over, quietly expected to make peace with less. Despite it all, I kept showing up, doing the work, praying, and trusting that the story God was writing for me was far from complete.

The beautiful thing about walking with God is that even when you're weary, your steps are never in vain. The grind, the grace, and the growth were all working within me, refining me and teaching me to trust both the process and the One who sees it all. So, by the time another position opened in our division, I had already made peace with the idea that, even if it didn't come through, I would be okay.

This one felt different. It was a position in the Child and Adult Care Food Program (CACFP), the same area that had recalled me after the RIF. The posting was under a different supervisor. When I asked the director about the position, her voice was calm, almost warm. She told me it was a position she believed I should apply for.

I didn't know what moved her to say it. Maybe she had been watching me. Perhaps time had softened something within her. Or maybe she had come to realize what I had always known, that I was already carrying leadership within me. That I didn't need a title to show up as someone truly invested. My director's encouragement could have landed like irony, but instead, it landed like redemption. It didn't erase the past, but it did speak powerfully to the present.

There's something incredibly healing about being seen by someone who once dismissed you. It wasn't about her approval. I had long since stopped chasing that. It was about God showing me, through the most unlikely vessel, that my time had not passed; that He hadn't forgotten what I had sown.

So, I took a breath, prayed over it, and applied. The role was a counterpart to my previous position, the one my supervisor had fought to get me back from. When my prior supervisor campaigned for me to return to her area, I felt a sense of pride. She valued me, wanted me back, and had no problem making her desires known to anyone who would listen. I wanted to go back, too. I liked the comfort and ease I'd known before the RIF, so I wanted her to succeed in getting me back. Here I was, applying to return to the area that recalled me.

Sometimes, we settle for where we are supposed to be and make comfortable decisions rather than informed ones. We can go off track, and circumstances can disrupt our comfort, redirecting us.

The job came with a slight pay increase, so this move wasn't about money. This decision was about growth, stretching, and stepping into something new without the safety of comfort. I knew what it meant to accept a position that didn't come with immediate gain. I also knew what it felt like to be stagnant. More than anything, I was determined not to settle. I had learned that sometimes elevation comes disguised as a sidestep, that obedience and opportunity don't always look glamorous at first.

What the job offered was potential: a chance to grow new skills, an opportunity to lead in ways that aligned more closely with my heart, a chance to move beyond survival and into vision, finally. I wanted to contribute differently, and I knew I could.

While others may have looked at the position and seen more work for nearly the same pay, I saw an open door. I saw a purpose calling me forward, and I answered. I didn't step into that role timid or apologetic; I stepped in carrying lessons in my pocket and strength in my spirit. I had already learned how to lead without a title, and I had endured betrayal yet held fast to my integrity.

This time, I unapologetically carried all of that with me, my whole self, and more than that, my reason. This wasn't just about a position; it was about walking in alignment with who I was called to be. It was about reclaiming what had once been denied, not out of bitterness, but from a place of bold courage. I know that when God opens a door, especially one that others have tried to keep closed, no force is strong enough to shut it.

This wasn't just a promotion in duties; it was a promotion in perspective. A turning point where I was not merely seen, but established. This time, when I received the job offer, it felt like a return not to where I had been, but to who I had always been becoming.

The position was with the Child and Adult Care Food Program (CACFP), and though the title was new to me, the work didn't feel unfamiliar. It felt like the return of an old friend. From my first job in public service, food assistance had been a constant thread woven through my work. For most of my life, I had stood at the intersection of food and dignity. Working in the CACFP felt like another brushstroke in a masterpiece on a canvas I hadn't even realized was being painted.

The more I learned about the Child and Adult Care Food Program (CACFP), the more I saw my heart in its work. It wasn't glamorous. It wasn't loud. It was purposeful, rooted in advocacy and anchored in care. The program ensured that infants and preschool-aged children in daycare, along with elders in adult care facilities, received meals that met both federal and state guidelines. It was about more than food; it was about protection, equity, and nourishment for those who often couldn't advocate for themselves.

I stepped into that role not just with qualifications, but with a sense of sacred responsibility. I knew what hunger looked like, not in theory, but in memory. I remembered depending on school meals, counting pennies to buy groceries, and praying over an empty fridge. When I reviewed documents from a daycare center, I didn't just see paperwork; I saw children whose well-being depended on someone taking the time to get it right. When I monitored a facility, I didn't just walk in as an evaluator; I walked in as a protector of those who are often unseen.

One of my first visits was to a small childcare center near a church. The children were lively and playful, their joy radiating through their drawings and the songs they sang. I remember watching lunch being served and the excitement on those little faces as they ate. I watched a little girl fold her hands in prayer before taking her first bite, and my eyes filled with tears.

Chapter 22: Don't Ignore the Sparks

It brought me back to my childhood with striking vividness, days when the only hot meal came from school or a state-funded summer program, days when the rumble of the meal truck was the sound of relief. As I stood there, surrounded by chattering toddlers and patient teachers, something in me healed. The little girl I once was, who had received a meal handed to her in love, was now making sure someone else's child didn't go without.

The thing about God's redemptive work is that it's never solely about the moment. His redemption is about connection, restoration, and the full-circle fulfillment of what once felt broken or forgotten.

In staff meetings and audits, I spoke up more, not because I was louder, but because I was surer. This job gave me reason to reclaim parts of myself I had allowed to dim. My voice mattered here. My instincts mattered. I saw how my lived experience sharpened my professional presence. I brought empathy into every conversation, order to every file, and vision to every review because I wasn't just working a job; I was building a legacy. I was making sure children could eat and caregivers could trust. I was helping uphold something sacred in systems that are too often overlooked.

This job was also personal. It was a reclaiming of my voice, silenced by disappointment but never extinguished. A reclaiming of my worth, the kind that doesn't need validation because it's been carved through years of faithful service. A reclaiming of my belief that I belonged in the rooms where policies are shaped, systems are formed, and outcomes are decided.

This time, I didn't need to be invited to the table to know I belonged there. I brought my own seat. And, more importantly, I brought substance.

In CACFP, I wasn't just auditing meals; I was helping preserve the kind of dignity that lasts beyond a lunch tray. I was feeding futures. And in doing so, I was nourishing my own sense of purpose in ways I hadn't even known I was hungry for. With every child I saw eating well, with every elder receiving care, I whispered to my soul: I may have been rejected, dismissed, and overlooked, but I have not been defeated.

I did not crumble under the weight of disappointment, nor did I allow bitterness to take root. I kept moving forward, one faithful step at a time. I had done the work. I showed up on the days it was hard to smile, the days I questioned if it was worth it, and the days I wanted to quit. I leaned on grace when my strength was gone, walked in integrity when no one was watching, and then the door opened.

The door opened because I never gave up. Divine favor made room for me, the kind that doesn't ask for permission, flows from faithfulness, and opens doors no one can shut.

What made it even more divine was discovering that this new area oversaw the Summer Food Service Program (SFSP), a detail I hadn't fully grasped until I was already in the role, hearing the full scope of responsibilities. When I listened to the words "summer meals for children," my breath caught in my throat. It was as if a vision from my past had returned.

I conducted on-site reviews for the SFSP whenever additional help was needed. I visited community sites, churches, libraries, parks, and apartment complexes where children gathered for summer meals and activities. I watched little faces light up as they opened cartons of milk and unwrapped sandwiches. I heard the laughter of kids playing as volunteers looked on.

Those moments stirred vivid memories. I remembered the rumble of the meal truck pulling up to the church where we held VBS when I was a child. I remembered standing in line, paper bag in hand, excited to receive a meal from my mother's smiling face. I remembered the relief in my mother's eyes, knowing that for at least one more day, her children were fed.

Now, I was the one ensuring those trucks rolled in, the meals met nutritional guidelines, and the children received not just food, but dignity. The weight of that full-circle moment was almost too much to hold.

There were days I sat quietly in my car after a site visit and wept not out of sadness, but in awe. Look at what God has done, how He took the little girl who once needed help and made her the woman who now ensures others receive it.

This role opened fresh opportunities. I began connecting with new networks of professionals, nutrition experts, educators, and community leaders. My understanding of federal and state programs deepened, and I joined in policy conversations. My name appeared in email chains I'd never seen before. People began seeking my input, not merely because of my title, but because they had witnessed the results of my work.

More than the visibility or professional growth, something inside me began to shift. I gained a new clarity and boldness, not the kind that pushes people aside, but the type that knows how to take rightful space without apology.

In this season, I realized something critical: leadership isn't just about being in charge. It's about impact. It's about presence. It's about empathy and the kind of wisdom that can't be taught in a training, but cultivated in the soil of lived experience.

In every classroom I visited, every child I greeted, and every administrator I trained, I brought more than policy knowledge. I brought my story, my walk, my tears, and my triumphs. I didn't tell them what I had been through; I led from it. I showed up with a depth born of overcoming. This wasn't just a chapter in my career; it was a turning point in my life.

This was about legacy and mentoring others, about widening the path for the next person. It was about showing up in meetings and community centers alike with the conviction that what we do matters, and that how we treat people along the way matters even more. I wasn't just climbing a ladder; I was leaving a roadmap and adding extra rungs as I went, narrowing the distance between each step so others could climb without losing heart.

Chapter 23: A Leader Is Born

By 2008, a clarity so profound and undeniable had settled within me that it nearly startled me. I realized I had been created to train people.

Training wasn't just a skill I had picked up. It was intrinsic, woven into the fibers of my being. Every time I trained, something inside me came alive: a sense of impact, a natural rhythm, and the conviction that what I was doing mattered far beyond the day's checklist.

When I stood before childcare professionals, breaking down federal guidelines and answering their questions, I didn't feel like I was just explaining policy. I felt like I was empowering them, helping them live out their callings with greater confidence. That mattered to me in ways I hadn't fully understood until then.

I began to see that everything I had done, long nights learning unfamiliar systems, quiet disappointments, and years of staying faithful without recognition, had been preparing me for something far more profound.

If I were honest, I had known it all along. Back when I first enrolled in college, my heart was set on becoming a teacher. I wanted to be in classrooms, shaping lives, helping people see their potential. But life brought interruptions, unexpected turns, family obligations, financial strain, and a weariness that made the dream feel like a luxury. Survival and providing for my family took priority, and in the process, I quietly set that dream aside.

I came to learn that dreams don't age or die. They wait patiently, faithfully, until we are strong enough and whole enough to embrace them again. So, when I felt that old fire flicker back to life, I paid attention. I didn't dismiss it or push it back down. I leaned into it.

That's when I applied for a formal training position within the agency. This was more than just another job. It was the first intentional step toward the calling I now fully recognized. I was nervous, but I was also ready to be a trainer, to lead, to pour into others, to build systems, and to empower people.

A position opened up in our training department. The role focused on training employees in the very areas where I worked on the front lines. I applied with excitement, but I wasn't selected.

This "no" struck differently, not because I hadn't heard it before, but because this time I felt a deep sense of alignment. This wasn't about building a career; it was about answering a calling and stepping fully into something I was created for.

Still, I didn't unravel. I had matured enough to understand that every "no" isn't a denial. It might simply be a delay. And sometimes God's "not now" is His deeper form of protection.

So, I kept moving. I kept growing. I kept preparing. I kept showing up as if the door had already opened because in some ways, it already had. Purpose had been awakened, and that awakening itself was a breakthrough.

Not long after, the agency launched the Leadership Development Institute (LDI), a program designed to equip, mentor, and elevate the agency's next generation of leaders. The moment I heard the description, I knew it was a perfect fit for me. I was overjoyed when my acceptance letter arrived.

This leadership program felt like divine timing. I embraced the opportunity wholeheartedly. I poured myself into every session, every assignment, and every late-night moment of reflection. I knew that if I wanted to lead in the future, I needed to be developed in the present.

One of the most impactful parts of the LDI was being paired with my mentor. She was exactly who I needed in that season, carrying wisdom without ego and gentleness without passivity. I'll never forget one of the assignments she gave me. She instructed me to ask five people I had great relationships with and five I didn't have such easy relationships with a single question: "When you hear my name, what comes to mind?"

It was one of the most vulnerable exercises I had ever attempted. It terrified me and transformed me at the same time. I was both surprised and humbled by what I discovered about myself. The people I assumed didn't think well of me offered the kindest, most affirming words, while some I believed were impressed with me shared constructive feedback I might never have received without that assignment.

That experiment became a mirror reflecting both the truth of who I was and the potential of who I could become. I journaled their responses and compared them to my own self-perception. I asked myself where I was in alignment and where I still needed to grow. Most importantly, I made space for grace in the process.

She didn't just guide me; she called me higher. She reminded me that training was teaching, that I didn't have to abandon my old dreams to fulfill my current assignments. God was blending the education I desired, the systems I understood, and the faith I carried into something uniquely mine.

On December 15, 2010, I walked into the final gathering of our leadership cohort and walked out a graduate of the South Carolina Department of Social Services' Leadership Development Institute. Receiving that certificate was more than a professional milestone; it was something tangible I could hold onto and cherish.

It was a reintroduction to a part of myself I thought I'd lost and a validation that I wasn't imagining things when I believed there was more for me. That certificate reminded me that every detour and disappointment had been leading me to this very place and this moment in my life.

Chapter 24: The Long Way Home

Not long after graduating from the Leadership Development Institute, that familiar whisper stirred in my spirit again as if to say, It's time to move on.

I had achieved much, weathered storms that tried to take me out, climbed ladders others thought I didn't belong on, and pushed through doors once slammed in my face, but even in my gratitude for where I stood, I knew there was more.

There were still dreams folded gently into the corners of my heart. Dreams of training. Dreams of building systems that didn't just meet compliance but transformed lives. Dreams of becoming a voice for those who, like me, had once been overlooked or underestimated. I had spent years pouring into others, and now I sensed God gently calling me to pour into myself again.

That call meant going back to school. I had graduated from Clemson University in 1994, a bright-eyed young woman trying to outrun poverty and prove to herself that she belonged. Now, 17 years later, I felt that same stretch but with deeper roots and a clearer reason.

Going back to school had always lived in my heart. I had long dreamed of earning my master's degree, but life has a way of convincing you that some dreams expire. As the years passed, working, getting married, raising a child, and helping keep a household afloat, I quietly assumed that door had closed. Until the day I decided it hadn't.

One day, I chose to believe again that the dream was still alive. I realized I didn't need everything perfectly aligned to take the next step. I just had to take it. So, with trembling faith and undeniable clarity, I applied to Clemson University's Master of Human Resource Development (MHRD) online program.

When the acceptance email landed in my inbox, I sat still and stared at it, letting the moment sink in. It felt as if I had just received a letter from my future self, the version of me who had never stopped believing, even when life tried to convince her otherwise.

And so, in 2011, I began the journey. I was working full-time, holding a part-time Certified Nursing Assistant (CNA) job at the local hospital, raising my son, loving my husband, and now juggling the demands of graduate school. There were late nights, early mornings, moments when fatigue pressed heavy, and days when my to-do list felt endless.

I wasn't chasing a degree to add another line to my list of accomplishments. I was living out my destiny. Every paper I wrote, every discussion I joined, every case study I analyzed felt like a brushstroke in the bigger picture God was painting in my life. I didn't yet know the full scope of what He was doing, but I could sense it. This wasn't just education; it was divine equipping for the journey ahead.

Even then, I knew this degree would open doors beyond the agency. I suspected I might not retire from the place I had once assumed would be my only stop. And I knew that obedience to purpose always leads to provision.

I was walking with purpose, head high, faith intense, eyes fixed on the road ahead. When I stepped onto Clemson's campus to graduate in August 2013, something in me stood a little taller. My steps felt grounded, deliberate, almost sacred. I had crossed many thresholds in my life, but this one was different.

This was never just an academic journey. It was a return to a sacred space in my story. I had once walked those same sidewalks as a scared, uncertain young woman crying in elevators, feeling unseen, mailing checks I didn't want to part with. I remembered scraping together borrowed money, eating ramen noodles, and pretending I wasn't struggling.

Now I was back, not broken, not begging, but bold. The girl who once walked in worn shoes to catch a bus, who curled up on a well-loved couch with noodles and tuna and prayed between tears, was now walking confidently across a stage, degree in hand, cloaked not just in academic regalia, but in the glory of it all.

Graduating was a testament to so many things. It was healing. It was a declaration that I had arrived, not because the road was easy, but because I never stopped walking it.

Graduating with my Master's was the moment I shifted from chasing validation and striving to prove my worth to rooms that never truly saw me, to standing firmly in truth, my truth, and God's truth about me. My degree didn't define me; it simply confirmed what had always been true: I was equipped, capable, and called.

Up until then, I had spent years merely surviving the job, the systems, the seasons of being overlooked, underpaid, and underestimated. I did the work. I carried the load. I wore resilience like armor because I had no other choice.

But now? Now I wasn't just working. I was preparing to shape my future, to lead with purpose, and to leave a legacy measured not by titles or accolades, but by the hearts I touched and the people I trained. This was the foundation I would build, one rooted in authentic leadership, clarity, and the ability to see purpose in what others overlook. It was about courage, the kind that dares to lead with heart, even when it comes at a cost. It was about calling the deep, unshakable pull that refuses to let you quit, even when every part of you wants to. And finally, I was ready to live it out loud.

No more shrinking. No more apologizing for dreaming big. No more waiting for permission to rise. I had learned that you don't need everyone to believe in you to move forward. What God has placed within you still matters. Your yes is powerful. Your journey with every high, every valley, every no, and every closed door carries meaning.

Graduating made me a two-time Clemson alum. I crossed that stage empowered, prepared, and determined to make the rest of my life a living reflection of God's grace.

Chapter 25: Leaving to Live

By 2013, I had spent seventeen years at the Department of Social Services (DSS), a place where I had grown, learned, and transformed. DSS had been the backdrop to some of my most significant personal and professional milestones. It was where I rebuilt my life after trauma, found my voice, climbed professional ladders, and broke generational barriers.

Then, something began to stir within me. It wasn't frustration or burnout, it was a gentle, persistent whisper, an inner unease that told me I had fulfilled what I was meant to do there. It was time to see what was next. The realization brought release, a divine nudge urging me toward the next chapter of my life.

Leaving DSS was not a decision I made lightly. I had envisioned retiring there, believing it would be my only career stop. I didn't know how to say goodbye to a place that had been such an integral part of my identity. Yet as days turned into weeks, the certainty grew stronger: I needed to explore what was next. My assignment was shifting both career-wise and spiritually.

I began seeking roles aligned with my passion for training and development. I wasn't interested in simply managing tasks; I wanted to teach, to pour into others, to multiply impact. I longed for a position where I could operate with purpose, not just occupy a title.

Two opportunities soon emerged. The first was with the South Carolina State Department of Education in the National School Lunch Program (NSLP), a sister program to the one I was already working in. The role was more than 50% field-based, offering flexibility and a meaningful extension of my work in child nutrition. It was a natural progression one that allowed me to transfer my knowledge while experiencing a new agency environment.

The second opportunity was with the University of South Carolina (U of SC) as a Training and Development Director, responsible for providing training to the SNAP staff at DSS. Interestingly, the training program at DSS had been eliminated and outsourced to the U of SC. It felt almost poetic that the very division I had once hoped to join, but wasn't chosen for, had now been reborn elsewhere, and they were inviting me to interview.

I interviewed for both roles within a tight timeframe.

The NSLP interview went well, and I was soon offered the position. At first, it felt like the perfect door had opened. The job aligned closely with my background in federal nutrition programs, particularly my years with the CACFP. It promised a sense of continuity while still offering a fresh environment, new colleagues, and a familiar mission, a bridge to the next version of myself.

Then I heard the salary. My heart sank. It was the very bottom of the agency's pay scale, a figure that didn't reflect my years of experience, the expertise I carried, or the leadership skills I brought. I paused, took a breath, and did what I knew how to do best: I advocated for myself.

I reached out, requesting a salary increase. I explained that I wasn't new to this work. I had walked the road, worn the shoes, understood the mission, and carried the weight of responsibility in similar programs. I wasn't asking for anything extravagant, just a fair reflection of the value I offered.

The answer came back: the salary was non-negotiable. The refusal stung. After years of service and unseen sacrifices, I was still being met with the bare minimum. I had hoped that this new season would bring affirmation, not just in words but in tangible value.

I sat with it. I prayed. And clarity came that my worth wasn't tied to their offer, but my direction was tied to God's plan. While I still believed my experience merited higher pay, I understood this was about more than a paycheck. The slight raise was still a step forward and an opportunity to grow. If I turned it down solely over salary, I would be letting money dictate my future rather than faith. With mixed emotions and quiet resolve, I accepted the job. This was about positioning myself for the path ahead.

On October 17, 2013, I submitted my resignation from my position with the Child and Adult Care Food Program (CACFP). I expressed my heartfelt appreciation to the agency, its leadership, and my colleagues for the growth, support, and journey we had shared. Sometimes, we say yes not because every detail aligns perfectly, but because we know it's simply time to go.

The goodbyes had already begun to take shape in my heart, and I was preparing to step into the next chapter with the National School Lunch Program. I had made peace with the salary. While it wasn't everything I had hoped for, it felt like progress, and that was enough.

I called one of the directors I had interviewed with at U of SC to let her know I had accepted another position. She was stunned. Their hiring decision, she explained, had been delayed by HR processing and logistical setbacks, none of which had anything to do with me. Her voice was warm, respectful, and steady as she continued. They had completed interviews, finalized deliberations, and reached a decision.

When she told me I was being recommended for the Training and Development Director position, I froze.

Chapter 26: The Message I Found

Her words hit me like a wave, soft yet unyielding. I had to sit down. My heart dropped in disbelief. The Training and Development Director position was the role I had dreamed of, one devoted to leading, training, and developing others. It perfectly aligned with my giftings and my Master's degree. This was a role I had prepared for not only with credentials, but through decades of lived experience.

I gently explained to her that I had already accepted another offer and that my resignation date was already set. I told her that if I heard from USC's HR in time, I would consider it. And I meant it. Because while my head urged me to stick with the safer choice, my heart was whispering something else. This wasn't just a job; it was a career. It was a purpose. It was divine alignment.

The USC interview process had been straightforward but challenging. First, I met with upper management in a structured, serious roundtable interview that balanced scrutiny with sincerity. Then I was tasked with designing and delivering a five-minute training session on an assigned topic.
I will never forget standing in that auditorium. The lights were bright, the seats narrow, and the space hummed with expectancy.

In the midst of it all, I began to speak, to train, and to do what I had always loved. Something within me caught fire.

I wasn't nervous. I wasn't guessing. I was in flow. That training wasn't just a sample of what I could do; it was a mirror reflecting who I was. Every detour, every rejection, every assignment I had taken with trembling hands and bold faith had led to that moment. I knew, deep in my bones, that this was where I belonged. That room didn't just hold possibility, it held destiny.

Still, nothing was coming easily, and there was one detail about the position that I could not overlook.
The position was temporary and grant-funded, offering at-will employment with no promise of longevity. During the October interview, the team was transparent: if funding for the next fiscal year weren't renewed, the role would end on July 1. It was a sobering truth, one that didn't fade beneath the glow of excitement.

This wasn't just about me. I had a husband, a child, and a household to care for. Losing my income wasn't something we could easily absorb. My responsibilities were greater than I'd ever imagined. And I had already accepted another offer, one that was stable and secure.
Changing course now felt dangerous. Risky. Even dishonorable. I didn't want to appear ungrateful to the agency that had opened a door for me when others hadn't. I didn't want to be seen as fickle or unsure.

But I was learning something in real time: faith often asks us to choose between the safe and the sacred, between comfort and calling. At that moment, I stood at a crossroads, with one road leading to safety and the other into the unknown.

One quiet morning, I drove to work with my thoughts in full collision. The streets were still, but inside, my mind was loud. I gripped the steering wheel, wrestling with a choice that could alter everything. My thoughts volleyed between logic and longing, between the known and the unknown, between safety and purpose.

I prayed for guidance. There was no booming voice from heaven. No sign, no billboard, no burning bush. Only a stillness and then a whisper in my spirit that wasn't my own: What have you always wanted to do?

The question startled me. I had been asking for an answer, not expecting a question. But that's how God works sometimes. He doesn't always hand us the solution. He redirects us to the truth He's already planted within.
I paused. And in that stillness, the answer surfaced
 not from logic, but from longing. It rose from the deepest part of who I was: I've always wanted to teach. To train. To lead people into growth and purpose.

That was it. No further instruction. No lengthy download from the divine. Just that one sacred whisper. God didn't say another word. He didn't need to.

The question had done its work. This wasn't about the job; it was about my journey. About the courage to choose purpose when everything around me made a convincing case for predictability. It was as if God Himself were asking, "Will you trust Me enough to choose the thing that speaks to your soul, even when it says nothing to your bank account or sense of security?"

A sobering truth stared me in the face: the U of SC job,

The one I had dreamed of, the one aligned with my calling, was temporary. Grant-funded. At-will. It could end in less than nine months, leaving me at square one job hunting again, with bills to pay and responsibilities to shoulder.

The National School Lunch Program position, on the other hand, was permanent familiar territory, simply an extension of the work I was already doing. On paper, it made perfect sense, offering a modest raise and the kind of stability any working wife and mother could depend on.

But it didn't stir my spirit. It didn't awaken the little girl in me who once dreamed of standing before classrooms, helping others see what was possible within themselves. It carried no echo of purpose. It was good, but in this moment, it wasn't mine.

I knew what I had to do. With a trembling kind of peace, I called the hiring manager at U of SC and accepted the offer. Then, with equal respect and humility, I contacted the State Education Department to rescind my acceptance.

I accepted the job with no guarantees, yes to the possibility that I'd be back on the job market in less than a year, yes to the vision that refused to leave me alone, yes to the voice that told me I was made for more.

Let me tell you what began as a temporary position became more than two years of growth, impact, and favor. The grant was renewed multiple times, and by the time it was finally discontinued, I had already moved on several years earlier. What once looked unstable on paper became the very launching pad of my purpose.

In that role, I had space to breathe and room to stretch. Going to work felt refreshing; it didn't feel like work, and it certainly didn't feel like stress. I developed training and facilitated sessions that not only informed but also transformed employees. I engaged with staff and agency leaders in ways that affirmed the fullness of who I had become. I was no longer merely surviving in a job; I was thriving. Thriving in my calling.

That season taught me that faith is rarely convenient, but it's always worth it. Sometimes, faith feels like shouting hallelujah from a mountaintop. More often, it's quiet courage behind the wheel of your car, whispering a trembling yes into the unknown.

I'm so glad I didn't let fear masquerade as wisdom. I'm so glad I didn't let the voice of security drown out the sound of my calling. And I'm grateful I never abandoned the little girl who once dared to believe her voice could make a difference, singing and speaking to the trees as if they were an audience.

When I honored that yes, doors didn't just open; they aligned, and that alignment became the beginning of everything that followed.

Chapter 27: Answering Your Call

There comes a time when you stop chasing a paycheck and start searching for purpose, for peace, and for alignment with who you've become.

By 2013, something more profound than ambition began to rise within me. I had climbed ladders, earned degrees, and found my voice in rooms where I once felt invisible. Yet beneath those accomplishments, a quiet call had been echoing for years, one I tried to ignore, outrun, and even negotiate with.

The callings we feel in life don't fade. They wait. They wait until we are ready to surrender, until the applause dies down and the only voice left is His. For me, that call was to preach not just to speak, but to declare.

Not just to teach, but to transform. Not just to be seen, but to serve in a way that would awaken others to their own purpose. I wrestled with it for years. I was scared.

Uncertain. Convinced I wasn't qualified. I had spoken on stages, led training sessions, and coached others. But this was different. This felt sacred in a way that demanded not just my skill set, but my whole self.

Eventually, I found the courage to speak with my pastor. I didn't walk into that conversation with a polished presentation; I walked in with trembling obedience. I told him I believed God had called me.

He said, "Okay." It wasn't rushed. Later, he returned and spoke the words that would change everything: "It's time."

So, I began the process training, preparing, and surrendering to a mantle I could no longer avoid. And in August 2013, the same month I graduated from Clemson with my Master of Human Resource Development, I stepped into the pulpit at Haskell Heights First Baptist Church and preached my initial sermon. The title was "Get Up" based on John 5:1-14, the story of the man at the pool of Bethesda.

When I look back, I realize my sermon wasn't only about biblical healing, it was my testimony. Like the man at the pool, I had waited for someone to see me.

Waited for the doors to open. Waited for the pain to ease. But Jesus doesn't wait for our confidence; He moves when we are ready to obey. "Do you want to be made whole?" That was His question to the man, and it was His question to me. My answer was a trembling yes.

That sermon was a mirror to see myself fully, not as the woman who had been overlooked or underestimated, but as the woman who had risen again and again.

Speaking of rising, I'll never forget the first suit I ever bought years ago. It was on clearance at Sears for $49. That might not sound like much to some, but to me, it was everything. I had dreamed of owning a suit not for vanity, but for dignity. I wanted to walk into rooms as if I belonged there. When I finally bought it, I didn't even feel worthy to wear it.

Standing in that pulpit, delivering a sermon born from my survival, I realized it was never about the fabric on my back; it was about the fabric of my faith. That day, I wore more than a suit. I wore every testimony God had stitched together in secret. I wore the memory of Walmart dresses and silent prayers. I wore resilience. I wore redemption.

I preached that sermon in the very church where I once sat quietly, wondering if I'd ever be good enough. I used to look at the pulpit as if it belonged to another world, untouchable. Now, I was standing in it, not because I had mastered anything, but because I had surrendered everything.

That sermon, "Get Up," became my mantra. It wasn't just an initial sermon; it was a roadmap I had been following and would continue to follow for the rest of my life, a mission to reach those who felt stuck. To remind them that God doesn't just visit the places we hide; He calls us out of them. He doesn't just comfort us in our waiting; He empowers us to walk.

Ministry is a platform I carry into boardrooms, training sessions, and every encounter where someone needs to be reminded of their worth. I was stepping fully into my assignment in leadership that flows from love, into purpose that refuses to play small, into a ministry that shows up not only on Sundays but in everyday moments for everyday people.

Every time I open my mouth to speak, to teach, or to preach, I remember the suit, the sermon, and the silence that came before the call.

And I still hear that quiet, steady voice whisper: "Get up."

Chapter 28: When Critique Meets Calling

I was beyond happy as a Training and Development Director. For the first time in a long while, work didn't feel like work; it felt like worship. It wasn't about the title or even the tasks. It was about alignment.
I had finally stepped into a space that fit me like a glove.

Every day, I felt I was using every gift God had given me, and none of it was going to waste.

Designing training. Developing curriculum. Facilitating conversations that moved people from confusion to clarity. Standing in front of a room, whether in person or online, and watching the light come on in someone's eyes. That was it for me. It was more than fulfilling. It was divine.

It felt as if all the years of detours, disappointments, and waiting had been quietly preparing me for this. I wasn't just operating in skill; I was living my calling. And it showed. But life has a way of reminding us that purpose doesn't make you immune. Walking in alignment doesn't mean you won't trip over the unexpected.

After facilitating a few sessions, I was scheduled to conduct my first extensive in-person training in this new role. I had trained many times before at DSS and at conferences, so I wasn't in unfamiliar territory. I arrived prepared, excited, and rooted in what I knew I had been waiting my whole life to do.

The training went well. The energy was alive, and the participants were engaged. We laughed, we learned, and we connected in meaningful ways. When it was over, I felt exhilarated—like I had poured myself out in the best way possible. I walked away already dreaming of how to make the next one even better.

And then, the evaluations came in. Most were precisely what I expected: positive, affirming, and grateful. Words like engaging, transparent, authentic, and inspiring leaped off the pages. But buried among them was one comment that pierced like a sharp weapon. It said I used too much humor and criticized what I wore. One comment on a page full of encouragement, and yet it stuck like a splinter under the skin of my confidence.

I don't know why it hit me so hard. Maybe because, deep down, I was still healing from years of being overlooked, and now the fear of rejection had surfaced again. Those written words wrapped around my spirit and began to squeeze. I started to doubt if I was as good as I thought. Maybe I didn't belong here after all.

I was devastated. I knew better, but knowing and feeling are two different things. In that moment, I felt crushed, wounded in a way that seemed far too real for the situation. I wanted to hide. I questioned everything. Was I too much? Too relaxed? Should I have toned it down? Worn something different?

It's wild how one comment can spark a war inside you, even after years of building peace.

My supervisor, who had watched me radiate all day with the joy of doing what I loved, noticed instantly that something had shifted. I had walked into that room earlier, standing tall in my calling, but now, something in me had deflated. My energy dulled. My smile dimmed. He quietly pulled me aside, not urgently, but with deep care. He didn't need explanations. I hadn't spoken a word, yet he could see it on my face: the self-doubt creeping in.

Then he spoke words that anchored me. "If you're going to stand in front of people," he said, "you have to learn to filter out the noise. Not every voice deserves a seat at the table of your identity."

He didn't say it like a pep talk; he said it like the truth. It wasn't theory, it was the voice of someone who had stood in more rooms, led more sessions, and weathered more storms than I could count. This wasn't advice; it was a lifeline. A sacred reminder that I didn't have to take everything personally. I could choose what to keep and release the rest.

The truth was, I had received over twenty evaluations that day, and only one was critical. Just one. Every other response had been glowing, praising the clarity of the content, the pacing, the interactive elements, and how the training not only informed but also inspired. And there I was, letting a single sentence drown out an entire symphony of affirmation.

That one person hadn't asked for more clarity. They hadn't requested extra support. Their critique wasn't even about what I taught; it was about how I delivered it. My personality. My expression. My presence

I was utterly devastated and crushed. I knew better, yet knowing and feeling are two very different things. In that moment, I felt wounded in a way that seemed far too real for the situation. I wanted to hide. I questioned everything: Was I too much? Too relaxed? Should I have toned it down? Worn something different?

It's wild how a single comment can ignite a war inside you, even after years of building peace.

My supervisor, who had watched me radiate all day with the joy of doing what I loved, noticed immediately that something had shifted. I had walked into that room earlier, standing tall in my calling, but now, something inside me had deflated. My energy dulled, my smile dimmed. He pulled me aside quietly, not urgently, but with deep care. He didn't need explanations. I hadn't spoken a word, yet he could see it on my face, the self-doubt creeping in.

Then he spoke words that anchored me: "If you're going to stand in front of people," he said, "you have to filter out the noise. Not every voice deserves a seat at the table of your identity."

He didn't deliver it like a pep talk; he spoke it as truth. It wasn't theory, it was the voice of someone who had led more sessions, stood in more rooms, and weathered more storms than I could count. This wasn't advice, it was a lifeline, a sacred reminder that I didn't have to take everything personally. I could choose what to keep and release the rest.

The truth: I had received over twenty evaluations that day, and only one was critical. Every other response had been glowing, praising the clarity of the content, the pacing, the interactive elements, and how the training informed and inspired. And there I was, letting a single comment drown out an entire symphony of affirmation.

That one person hadn't asked for clarity or requested extra support. Their critique wasn't about what I taught, it was about how I delivered it: my personality, my expression, my presence.

That's when something clicked: I hadn't failed to do my job. I simply hadn't aligned with someone's personal preference, and that was okay. You can give your absolute best, pour your soul into your work, and still not be everyone's cup of tea. Some people like humor in training because it creates warmth and relatability; others prefer strict formality. Some enjoy a personal touch, while others want just the facts, no frills. None of that makes your delivery wrong it simply means your style isn't for everyone.

In that moment, I realized that feedback is a gift. Like any gift, I get to decide what to keep and what to set aside. That evening, when I got home, I resisted the urge to spiral. I could have replayed that one comment over and over like a broken record in my mind. Instead, I did something different: I laid it at God's feet.

I told Him how it made me feel, how vulnerable I was, how hard I had worked, and how unfair it seemed that my confidence had been shaken. I realized I could not dim my light just because someone else wasn't comfortable with the voltage. I had spent years fighting to be seen, to be heard, and to walk fully in the purpose God had placed inside me. I would not shrink back now.

I couldn't minimize my joy to make others feel comfortable. I couldn't apologize for being me for bringing warmth, authenticity, and a little laughter into a space that, for many, was the only break in an otherwise heavy workweek. I was called to that room not by a committee, not by a hiring manager, but by purpose. The same God who opened the door would sustain me in that room.

That day taught me something I'll carry for the rest of my life. You can embrace critique without accepting condemnation. You can adjust without losing your essence, leading with both confidence and compassion, knowing that not every voice is meant to shape how you see yourself.

I walked into the next training a little wiser, a little stronger, still smiling and still joking. Still fully myself, because purpose doesn't come with permission slips, and the call on your life isn't up for a vote. I kept showing up with joy, with clarity, and with complete confidence that who I am and how I lead is not just enough but appointed. Joy is part of my anointing, and humor is part of my voice. Showing up as my whole, warm, bold self isn't a liability; it's a gift.

From that day forward, I kept showing up, this time with guardrails around my identity. I receive feedback, filter it through the lens of truth, and remain teachable. I stopped wavering because, in the end, the voice that matters most is the One who called me in the first place. He never said I had to be perfect, only that I had to show up. And I'm so glad I did.

That experience reminded me that leadership and visibility always invite scrutiny. Moments like that helped me grow. I was happy in my job, content enough that I could have stayed there forever. But I learned that contentment doesn't always mean your purpose is fulfilled. Something inside me began to stir a restlessness I had come to recognize over the years as a sign of transition. It wasn't fear or dissatisfaction; I knew change was coming.

It wasn't a loud shift, more like a soft hum that grew louder with each passing day. I began to sense that while I was walking with intention, I was also being prepared for a pivot. So, I did what I've always done in moments like that: I prayed and began looking for what was next, not in desperation but in discernment.

Then, one opportunity caught my attention. It was for a trainer position at another state agency. The program wasn't one I had worked in before, but the work itself felt familiar. It aligned closely with a program I had once partnered with, and as I read through the description, something inside me lit up. It sounded like an opportunity to grow, to stretch, and most importantly, to keep doing what I loved: training people with compassion, clarity, and confidence.

When I arrived for the interview, I stepped into the room and froze. Across the table sat a familiar face. It was my former supervisor, the one selected for the position I had once believed would be my promotion.

The interview unfolded like an easy conversation with old colleagues. There was ease, laughter, and respect. No awkwardness lingered, just a mutual acknowledgment that we all had a history and had handled it with grace. When I walked out of that room, I didn't feel heavy. I felt proud not of what I had said in the interview, but of how I had walked through the last several years. I had sown seeds of integrity, and now I was standing in the harvest of that character.

A few days later, the job offer arrived. There was confirmation that doing right, even when you've been wronged, never goes unnoticed by God. It wasn't about revenge. It wasn't about proving anything to them. It was about staying faithful and growing rather than becoming bitter or stagnant.

Then came the numbers. The salary they offered was noticeably lower than what I had requested. I took a breath and reminded myself of the prayer I'd prayed months earlier. I had told God I would move into a permanent position only if it came with at least a lateral salary. So, I countered respectfully, but boldly.

They responded with a modest increase, but it still fell short of the number God and I had agreed on. I wasn't negotiating from pride; I was standing on a promise. I knew what I carried, I knew my worth, and more than that, I knew what I had prayed for.

So, I said no, not out of arrogance, but out of alignment. I chose not to settle. I decided to believe that if God could open one door, He could open another. If the promise was "yes and amen," then I didn't need to twist my way into provision. Not long after that decision, another door opened that I never expected to see again.

The National School Lunch Program had posted a new position. It was the same agency I had accepted a role with two years earlier; the same one I had respectfully declined when the Training and Development Director role at USC became available. This time, the job description included training, and that detail caught my breath.

It felt as if the very thing I had once walked away from had returned. This time, it held my heart and calling in full view. It wasn't just another job posting; it felt personal, purposeful, like something that had been waiting for me to return, not in defeat, but in fullness.

When I changed directions back then, I communicated with clarity and respect. At the time, I had written a thoughtful email to the

HR department, explaining my decision and expressing sincere gratitude. Now, I applied without knowing whether they remembered me or if my previous declination would count against me.

My phone rang that Friday. It was someone from the NSLP administrative team. I could tell she was calling all prospective candidates for interviews, but the way she posed her question to me was unexpected. She asked something along the lines of whether I didn't want to interview. I told her I did, and she asked me to choose a time on Monday from her list of available slots.

I paused. Monday was tight. I was still working full-time, juggling responsibilities, and didn't feel fully prepared. I asked if another interview day was available. Her response came swiftly and firmly: Monday was the only day interviews would be held. If I declined, I'd have to wait and apply for another position.

I stood there, phone in hand, feeling the weight of the moment. This wasn't about scheduling; it was a test of obedience, of trust. A question of whether I'd let logistics keep me from stepping into what God was doing. I said yes. I didn't know how I'd make it work logistically. I didn't know what they'd ask or how it would go.

That weekend, my mind kept circling one lingering thought, the question I was sure they'd ask in the interview: "Why did you turn the job down before, and why should we trust you now?" No matter how I tried to focus on other possible questions or scenarios, that one loomed largest. It felt like a test I'd need to pass just to be considered. Instead of crafting a clever response or rehearsing answers, I resolved to be professionally honest and soulfully transparent. If they asked, I would tell the truth.

The first offer had come right after I earned my Master's degree, and the Training Director role aligned more directly with the training I felt called to. It wasn't about walking away from NSLP; it was about walking toward something I knew was divinely orchestrated. Years later, with more growth and a deeper understanding of my niche, I could see how this position still aligned with my purpose. Now, the scope had changed to include training.

On Monday, I walked into the interview room, took a deep breath, and prepared for whatever was ahead. To my surprise, nearly everyone from the previous panel was still there, plus one new face. The room felt familiar, settled, and anything but intimidating. There were no cold stares or side-eyed glances, only professionalism and genuine curiosity.

The question I had stressed over never came. They never asked why I had rescinded the previous job offer. Instead, the panel treated me as if I had always belonged in that room. They saw the fullness of my journey, not just a snapshot. And that, in itself, was healing.

A few days later, my phone rang, the offer was mine. Joy surged instantly, trailed by the inevitable follow-up question in my mind: But what about the salary? I had prayed about this long before I even applied. I knew the exact number I had committed to God in prayer.

I asked if there was any room to adjust the offer. The answer came back, no. It was less than $200 above my current salary, and with parking costs, it would essentially break even. Right there, in the middle of that conversation, God reminded me of the vow I had made: "Lord, if it's at least lateral, I'll go." And here it was lateral exactly as I had asked. God had kept His end of the agreement. I chuckled. God, you really do have a sense of humor. So, I said yes.

When I walked through the doors on my first day, it didn't feel like starting over. It felt like I had finally stepped into a place that had been waiting for me all along. I remember that day vividly. I parked several blocks away in a relentless downpour. As I spoke to a friend about how God had blessed me with the job at SCDE, he smiled and said, "You're the blessing, not the job."

From day one, everything clicked. The systems felt instantly familiar. The expectations were clear and straightforward. Several of the schools I supported were part of the CACFP, making the transition seamless. I didn't need months of orientation or handholding. I stepped in and got to work confident, steady, and focused. With roughly eight years until retirement eligibility, I made a promise to finish strong. To serve well. To leave things better than I found them.

Not long after leading a compliance review in a district, something unexpected happened. The district emailed my director to commend the experience, expressing genuine appreciation for my professionalism.

It was a small gesture, but it moved me deeply. Yet the real moment wasn't in the praise, it was in my director's response. She forwarded the email with a brief note: "I knew two years ago, during your first interview, that you'd be an asset to this team."

Tears welled in my eyes instantly. She hadn't forgotten me. She hadn't held my earlier decision against me. She had seen my worth from the very beginning, and in that moment, all the pieces of my journey seemed to snap into place. On the drive home, I could barely keep the tears from falling. All I could do was worship. Praise poured from my lips effortlessly because I had seen the hand of God so clearly, so gently, so faithfully over my life.

I thanked Him for keeping me through the loneliest seasons. For strengthening me when my heart lay broken. For covering my family when the finances made no sense on paper. For holding me through the "not yet" and the "not this time." Most of all, I praised Him for who He is to me, Faithful. Constant. A Father who never forgets.

I wept not out of sorrow but out of joy and deep relief. I finally understood that all those years of showing up, walking in obedience when it didn't make sense, giving when I barely had, sowing seeds in silence, none of it had been overlooked.

Then, in the stillness of that drive home, God spoke something into my spirit so personal, so specific that I will never forget it. He said, "I remember the candy bar."

The words took my breath away because I knew exactly what He meant. Years ago, when money was tight, and faith was all I had, I had to make ends meet, and I chose to keep tithing. I could have spent that money on movies, restaurants, or other little indulgences. But I trusted that provision would come because God is faithful, so I bought a candy bar, savored it, and waited.

It might have seemed small to anyone else. But it wasn't small when God saw it. He saw that candy bar. He saw the sacrifice. He saw the heart behind the offering. And now, all these years later, as I stepped into a role that carried both honor and responsibility, He reminded me He saw it then. He remembered. He never forgot my faithfulness.

I cried all the way home. Not tears of sadness, but of overwhelming gratitude. I cried because God never left me. I never stopped believing, sowing, or trusting. And He never stopped keeping His promises. Even when I felt overlooked, He had not forgotten me. He remembered the candy bar. He remembered me.

This role, in this season, wasn't just the fruit of my labor; it was the reward of obedience. It was the manifestation of grace. From that day forward, I led with a fresh awareness not only of my position, but of His presence.

God doesn't just open doors; He ordains them. And when you walk through one that He has opened, you walk in with peace, with purpose, and with praise.

Within a year, our team lead left for a promotion. I stepped into the interim role, and with the support of a new director who saw my leadership with fresh eyes, I was soon officially promoted to Team Lead. Three years later, when our director moved on, I was appointed Interim Director of the Office of Health and Nutrition at the South Carolina State Department of Education.

Not long after, the interim title was removed. I stepped fully into the role overseeing the entire K–12 Child Nutrition Program for the State of South Carolina, which now also included the Summer Food Service Program that had previously been housed at DSS. Let that sink in.

The girl who once stood in line with a blue lunch ticket, signaling that her meals were free. The girl who quietly prayed no one would look down on her when she saw other students with lunches from home. The girl who remembered what cold milk tasted like on a sweltering summer day because it was part of her lifeline.

That same girl was now leading the very program that once filled her physically and emotionally.
This wasn't just a job. This wasn't just a promotion. This was destiny and redemption.

Every policy I approved, every training I developed, every decision I made, I filtered through the lens of that little girl.

I made decisions for hungry children.

For the child who felt invisible in the lunch line.

For the school staff forced to do more with less.
For the families who relied on that tray of food to give their child a fighting chance to learn.
I led with empathy. I led with memory. I led with a mission.

And the lesson the full-circle truth I now hold is this: purpose never forgets your name.
Not when you've been overlooked.

Not when life detours you to places you never planned to go.
Not when the waiting wears you down and the silence makes you wonder if God still sees you.
He does. And purpose does too.

Because purpose isn't fragile, it doesn't expire. It doesn't fold under the weight of delay or rejection.
It waits with intention. It watches you become.
It watches you surrender.

It watches you keep showing up tired, faithful, unfinished, and it holds space for the version of you that's rising in the process.
Then, when the time is right, not your time, not their time, but God's appointed time, He doesn't just open a door.

He calls your name.

Not who you were.

Not as the person still second-guessing themselves.

But as the one who endured.

The one who grew in the dark.

The one who learned how to steward pain and carry purpose with power.

When that moment comes, you don't just walk through the door; you rise.

With authority. With clarity. With the quiet fire of someone who knows who they are and why.

When God brings it full circle, it feels like a promise fulfilled.

And that, my friend, is the kind of victory no man can take from you.

Part V: Stepping Into the Call

When Obedience Becomes Overflow

Here's where my story begins to sound like ministry because it is. When I surrendered my plans and finally said yes to my purpose, I began to see the fruit of seeds planted years earlier. It was all about alignment. When God aligns you with your assignment, even the smallest steps take on sacred significance.

Chapter 29: Starting Something New

While leading a statewide program, a familiar question began to echo in my spirit: What comes next? Not just after retirement but after everything. After the titles, the meetings, and the endless performance reviews. What legacy would I leave? How would I spend the years ahead not merely working, but creating a lasting impact?

I refused to fade quietly into retirement. I longed to give to the world in a way that drew from the deepest places of my soul.

Then came 2020, the year everything changed. The pandemic didn't just shake the world; it brought grief, uncertainty, and an unexpected stillness. A divine pause. The kind that forces you to notice what you've ignored, feel what you've suppressed, and confront truths you thought could wait.

In that stillness, something began to stir. I came face-to-face with a truth I could no longer outrun: I hadn't endured everything I had just to keep it hidden in silence.

Not the trauma. Not the betrayal. Not the ache of rejection. Not the way I clutched my son when everything else seemed to fall apart. Not the whispered prayers on bus rides, the tears I wiped on my sleeve before stepping into the office, or the victories too sacred to share. None of it was wasted, and none of it was meant to be hoarded.

Then I realized something sobering: my story wasn't mine to keep. It was mine to release to give, to pour, to plant like seeds in the hearts of those who felt forgotten, unworthy, or too broken to begin again.

That's when the dream rose not as a fleeting idea, but as a calling. It didn't knock politely. It didn't wait for me to feel ready. It came on intensely, unrelenting, and it refused to let me rest until I said yes.

For years, I felt the pull to speak life, to teach truth, to create safe spaces for those navigating emotional fatigue, spiritual uncertainty, or professional burnout. Now, it was time to build it. Amid a global crisis, as the world spun in uncertainty, I took my first steps toward what I believed would become one of the most significant chapters of my life.

I launched a vision. I gave it a name, not just a brand, but a declaration: D.W. Davis Consulting, LLC, also known as Donna Davis Presents. Not a performance. Not a production. But a presentation of truth.

Donna Davis presents healing. Donna Davis presents worthiness. Donna Davis presents resilience and restoration. Donna Davis presents you whole and empowered. I made it official by registering my company: D.W. Davis Consulting, LLC.

I opened a business bank account, heart pounding, hands shaking, smiling when the banker asked what kind of deposits I expected. "Honestly," I said, half-joking yet entirely truthful, "it might be a long time before any money gets in here."
The banker smiled gently. "That's perfectly fine."

And just like that, the foundation was laid not only of a business, but of a ministry, a movement, a safe space for truth-telling and soul work. D.W. Davis Consulting, LLC was intentionally born from everything I had walked through and everything I believed others could overcome.

If I could rise from the depths, reclaim my voice after silence, and trade survival for joy, career for calling, then I could help others do the same. I was talking about transformation. I began building my platform slowly, intentionally, and with sacred urgency.

In the beginning, I didn't have a business coach or a social media strategist. I didn't have fancy backdrops or high-tech equipment. What I did have was conviction, a smartphone, and a lifetime of experiences that had shaped my voice and deepened my faith.
So, I started small. I showed up on social media not with gimmicks or trends, but with the truth. I went live biweekly, heart pounding, palms sweating as I shared what God had placed on my heart. Sometimes it was a word of encouragement; other times, a story, a lesson, or a Scripture that had carried me through. I posted reflections on faith, identity, purpose, perseverance, and emotional healing.

It felt raw. Personal. Exposed. Speaking into a camera with no assurance anyone was watching was its own kind of faith walk. Many times, no one was. The live count sat at zero. The comments remained empty. The virtual room stayed silent.

I spent hours preparing, writing notes, reading Scripture, rehearsing my words, and praying over what to say. I'd sit in my dining room, phone propped up, lighting barely right, nerves rattling. Then I'd hit "Go Live," pour out everything I had, and end the video with no sign anyone had heard me.

I'd close the laptop, sink into the couch, and let out a deep sigh. I'd stare into the quiet, wondering if I had heard God wrong, wondering if anyone was listening, or if I had waited too long to start.

Whenever I felt like pulling back, shrinking down, or quitting, God breathed life into my weariness. Sometimes through a stranger. Sometimes through a friend. Always right on time.

Then a message would arrive: "Your post helped me more than you know." "I don't normally comment, but I needed that word today." "Thank you. Please don't stop."

Those words weren't just kind, they were confirmation. They were divine reminders that even when the room looked empty, hearts were still being filled. One of those reminders still brings tears to my eyes.

A middle school classmate, someone I hadn't seen in decades, called me out of the blue one night as I contemplated giving up. No small talk. No buildup. Just a word from the Spirit:

"God told me to sow into your business every month. I don't need details. I don't need updates. I know He said to give."

And she did. For over three years, she sent a monthly seed faithfully, quietly, without strings. She never asked for a service in return. In fact, she hired me as her life coach and insisted on paying for it.

She told me, "You may need an outfit for an event. You may need rest. You may need to buy groceries, gas, or peace of mind. I'm not sowing into your content; I'm sowing into your calling."

You know what's wild? The very first amount she sent matched the cost of that olive-green suit I had bought years ago, the first real suit I had ever purchased, the one I hesitated to wear because I didn't feel worthy. It was as if God whispered again: "See? I remember."
Every seed. Every sacrifice. Every moment you believed, even when nothing around you said it was working.

Through my business, I began to expand my vision. I became a certified life coach after a dear friend pointed out that I had always been coaching people. I began speaking professionally, facilitating workshops, and creating spaces where women could breathe again, where their stories were welcomed, their strength honored, and their voices reclaimed.

I didn't coach from theory alone. I coached from the trenches.

I had lived in shame, navigated burnout, cried on bathroom floors, and smiled through meetings. I had shown up when I didn't feel ready, believing in others long before I fully believed in myself.

When I sat across from a woman who felt stuck, who didn't know who she was anymore, who had done everything for everyone else, and wondered when her turn would come, I didn't offer clichés. I offered my heart, her truth, my presence. I knew what it felt like to wonder if you were too late, too old, too broken, too ordinary, or simply too tired. But I also knew what it meant to rise anyway.

My business became more than a platform; it became a ministry for the modern soul. For the ones who lead by day and cry by night. For the ones who raise families while carrying silent battles. For the ones who feel called to more yet fear the weight of the next yes. I built spaces not just to teach, but to stand with them.

My lived experience carried me, but I also grounded my coaching in proven methodologies, earning certifications in root cause and neuro-transformation. I knew deep down that if God could do it for me, He could do it for them, too.

I didn't show up on camera because I had to; I showed up on purpose. My sessions weren't about having it all together; they were about telling the truth, naming what we hide, and standing in the mirror to see ourselves through God's eyes, not the ones shaped by shame, scarcity, or smallness.

It was never just about telling my story; it was about helping others find theirs. The enemy loves it when we stay silent, when we bury our brilliance, when we hide our light out of fear or guilt. I had already done that, and now I was on a mission to pull others into the light.

Starting my business set me free. It gave me a voice, turned my pain into purpose, and permitted others to rise. So yes, my business was born in a storm. It became a shelter, a spark, a signpost declaring: You're not too late. You're just getting started.

Chapter 30: God Restores Even the Smallest Wounds

Some wounds don't scream. They whisper. And even in their quietest moments, God hears every word.

Some wounds don't arrive with loud cries or visible bruises. They live quietly, buried deep in the corners of the soul, tucked beneath layers of accomplishment, faith, and perseverance.

You think you've moved on. You have in your career, calling, healing, and growth. But now and then, a part of your past leans in and whispers, "I'm still here."

For me, it was the pain of childhood bullying. I thought I had made peace with it. I believed I had processed the hurt, forgiven those involved, and moved forward. I learned how to stand tall in rooms where I once felt invisible. I had overcome so much. But the truth is, sometimes the body grows up and moves on long before the soul catches up.

Growing up with strabismus, being called cross-eyed made me different. And to children, different often means target. I was teased relentlessly. The jokes came quick and sharp:

"Who are you looking at?"
"Can you even see straight?"

I heard those words more times than I can count, and each time, a little more of my self-worth chipped away.

I was often alone on the playground, sitting quietly while others ran in circles of laughter and friendship. I wasn't invited. I was omitted. I wasn't seen in the way I longed to be seen.

I was pointed at, mocked, and laughed at. I was called names I've tried to forget, names that still linger in the shadows of memory. I was excluded from games, shunned in the lunchroom, and made to feel like I didn't belong, not just because of how I looked, but because of who I was.

So, I learned to cope. I smiled even when it hurt. I stayed quiet. I shrank. I buried the ache beneath straight A's, polite manners, and silent prayers that someone would truly see me, not my eyes.

I grew up. I survived those years, or so I believed. I went on to achieve, to rise, to lead. I became the kind of woman people admired: resilient, composed, driven.

Here's the thing about childhood wounds: they don't always disappear. They sink deep into your subconscious. They grow roots. They quietly shape the way you move through life, how you enter rooms, how you interpret silence, how you brace yourself for rejection, even when no one is pushing you away.

I had buried the rejection so thoroughly that I convinced myself I had healed. But in truth, I had only normalized the pain. I wore my scars like armor, never realizing the wounds beneath were still open.

Because brokenness, when it's all you've ever known, can begin to feel like wholeness.

But God is continually working to lead us to the truth. He knows the right time. He knows when you're finally strong enough to revisit the hurt, not to relive it, but to release it.

That moment came for me on May 29, 2024.
The day began like any other. I was sipping tea, checking my email, and moving through my morning. Nothing out of the

ordinary. Until a message came through my phone that made my hands still in mid-scroll.

It was from a former classmate, someone I hadn't seen or spoken to in decades. The words were powerful. The heart behind them was healing.

"GM Donna. This is your classmate, _____. You are in my thoughts and prayers this morning. As I read my devotional from Our Daily Bread, it referenced Ephesians 4:29-32, emphasizing the importance of being kind and compassionate. I reflected on how unkind I was to you as far back as elementary school. I know God has forgiven me, and I pray for your forgiveness too. I wonder if there were any emotional scars? If so, I want to remove mine. You have persevered and become a beautiful, successful woman and a woman of God. I know this is out of the blue, but the Lord touched my heart this morning to reach out to you."

I read it once. Then again. And again. And then, I cried.
I wept not just because someone apologized, but for the little girl who never got the apology. The girl who sat alone in the lunchroom. The girl who avoided eye contact so she wouldn't be mocked. The girl who longed for just one day to feel like she wasn't the joke.
And suddenly, she was seen. Decades later. Not forgotten. Not ignored. Seen.

I wept for all the years I carried the pain in silence, convinced no one even remembered what I had lived through. And here, in the middle of an ordinary Wednesday morning, God orchestrated an extraordinary healing.

Not only did this person remember, but the Holy Spirit moved them to reach back in time and make it right. I sat with my face in my hands and whispered, "Thank you, Lord. You didn't forget me."

It wasn't about vengeance or vindication. It was about validation. It was about divine timing.

That message unlocked something sacred in me. It reminded me that God never forgets the tears we cry when no one's watching. He doesn't overlook the ache in our hearts, even when we wear our brightest smile. He bottles every tear. He sees every lonely moment. And at just the right time, He redeems it.

As I sat there, tears running down my face, praise rising from my soul, God spoke something I will never forget:

"I remember the candy bar."

In that moment, I knew He was telling me He remembered every seed I had sown. He remembered my sacrifices. He remembered my silence. He remembered my giving, my praying, my hoping. He remembered me.

That day wasn't just a healing. It was a holy appointment, a full-circle moment only God could orchestrate. The little girl who once felt invisible was now being invited into restoration.

It reminded me of something I want to remind you of:
No wound is too old for God to heal.
No scar is too deep for God to touch.
No memory is too painful for God to redeem.

He sees you. He loves you. And yes, He remembers.
In that moment, as I sat with my phone in hand and tears streaming down my cheeks, I felt something shift in the atmosphere like God Himself had reached back through time and gently taken the hand of the little girl I used to be.

The girl who walked school hallways feeling small and unwanted. The girl who carefully arranged her face each day to hide the hurt inside. The girl who whispered prayers: "Can you please just let someone sit with me today?"

God was reaching for her.
Not just the grown woman I had become but the wounded child I had once been. The child who carried rejection like a permanent backpack. The one who never asked for much just not to be mocked. Just to be seen.

To belong. Not just the grown woman I had become but the wounded child I had once been. The child who carried rejection like a permanent backpack. The one who never asked for much just not to be mocked. Just to be seen. To belong.

Chapter 31: Healed In Plain Sight

And in that sacred moment, she was finally embraced. She didn't need a crowd; she required that text. More than that, she needed to know someone had finally looked back and truly seen her. The healing didn't come with fanfare; it came quietly. In those tears, something holy was restored.

God wasn't just healing my mind or soothing my heart. He was working deep within my soul, reaching into layers I didn't know were still tender. He was making me whole from the inside out, from the beginning to the present.

That's the kind of healing only God can do. It reminded me that you can rise and still need restoration. You can lead and still need love to reach back and gather the parts of you left behind. You can be called and still carry wounds from when you were trying to belong.

When I finally gathered my thoughts, I responded to my classmate with the kind of grace healing makes possible, not from a place of bitterness, but from a beauty forged through pain and redemption.

"Thank you so much. You have no idea how much this means to me. I've forgiven you and others. God has healed those emotional scars. As children, we often don't realize how we affect each other; however, we can train the next generation to do better. Thank you for speaking to the earlier version of me. She needed that. I am saved and a minister, and God used you to restore what the enemy tried to destroy."

And I meant every word. Here's what I've learned: healing doesn't always come in therapy sessions or altar calls, though they have their place. Sometimes, healing comes through the obedience of someone willing to make amends. Sometimes God sends a whisper through a text message. Sometimes your restoration rides on the back of someone else's repentance, and that, too, is grace.

Only God could do that. Only God could take a decades-old wound, bring it full circle on an ordinary Wednesday morning, and heal it. Only God could turn silence into a song. Only God could transform a painful memory into a testimony, and isn't that just like Him?

To restore what you forgot was broken.
To redeem what you thought was buried.

To touch what you never believed could be healed.
He doesn't just fix the loud, visible things. He pursues the quiet places, the dusty corners, the hallway memories, the name you were once called that still lingers when you walk into certain rooms. He goes there because He loves you that deeply.

And here's what I know now: if He can heal me from that, He can heal you too. So, if you've ever wondered whether that part of your story is too small, too old, or too forgotten for God to care about, let this moment remind you God remembers, God redeems, and God restores.

He doesn't just want to heal the person you are today; He wants to hold the little child you once were and whisper: "You were never invisible to Me."

So let Him in. Let Him love the child in you until they no longer have to hide. Let Him speak life to the version of you that never got the apology. Let Him do for you what no one else knows how to do.

Healing isn't just about getting over the pain; it's about becoming whole enough to remember without weeping, to tell the story without trembling, to answer not from the wound, but from the wholeness. And when you heal that deeply, you don't just walk forward, you soar.

Chapter 32: God's Business Plan

Starting my own business was more than an entrepreneurial leap; it was a spiritual offering. I didn't launch a brand for applause, analytics, or bottom-line profits. I was answering a divine nudge that wouldn't let me stay silent. From the very beginning, I told God, "This is Your business," and I meant it. Every flyer, every coaching session, every workshop, every word spoken, I saw it all as sacred work.

So, when people looked at me sideways and asked why I kept going, why I kept showing up online, investing time, money, and energy without a visible return, I had a simple answer: "It's God's business, not mine. My job is to be faithful."

There were seasons when income was scarce and the return seemed invisible. Moments when bills loomed large and resources ran thin. I remember walking through my home, whispering prayers like, "God... Your business isn't making any money." Like the widow with the oil, I discovered that faith never runs dry when God is your supplier. He always provided, sometimes through unexpected clients, sometimes through generous Sowers, and sometimes through nothing short of miracles.

I was in partnership with the Most High Himself. I wasn't building a platform; I was creating an altar, a space where people could encounter truth, healing, and hope. I trusted Him to lead, and He trusted me to steward what He placed in my hands.

Then came the question that shifted everything. One day, during my usual commute home, same route, same radio station, same winding thoughts, I felt a whisper so clear it stopped me mid-thought: "Can I have your day job too?"

I paused, heart racing. I knew it was God. My immediate response was hesitant: "God, I only have about four more years until retirement. I've got this under control." The whisper came again: "Can I have your day job too?" This wasn't about employment—it was about surrender.

It hit me like a wave. God was never after my titles, my job, or even my plans. He was after me, my trust, my obedience, my heart. Slowly, piece by piece, I surrendered what mattered most to me.

That day, I surrendered the job He had once so graciously given me. Not knowing what would come next, not knowing how the story would unfold. I joked with friends and colleagues that I no longer had a job. They all belonged to God.

Still, life carried on. Until another whisper came, this time, it was stronger. Clearer. Weightier.
"Retire."

At first, I pushed it aside. I tried to negotiate. Two more years, Lord. Just until I hit a particular mark, I had plans. I had a number in mind. I was working toward my timeline. Every time I considered staying longer, the idea felt heavy. Burdensome. Like wearing a coat that no longer fits.

God gently reminded me, 'You have already surrendered this.' So, I did what I always do when I'm scared. I prayed and in my usual honest, daughter-to-Father way, I asked Him for a revised retirement date, within 6 months of His request. And true to His character, He honored my request.

Chapter 33: Retirement Was Obedience

I had already begun paying down my consumer debt and was preparing to leap into my business without financial stability, because I had made peace with the truth: it's God's business and He is faithful.

When the time came, I submitted my retirement application. The room fell silent. People were shocked, some confused, some even asking, "But... why now?" I had no flashy plans, no roadmap, no guarantees, but I had peace. After nearly three decades in public service, peace mattered more than a paycheck.

On January 3, 2025, after twenty-nine and a half years of dedicated service to the State of South Carolina, I retired as State Director of the Office of Health and Nutrition, a program I had once depended on as a little girl. It was the same program that ensured I had a warm meal and a sense of normalcy during difficult times, the same program where I once stood in line holding a blue ticket that marked my meal as free.

Now, I was leaving as the one who had ensured that no child under my leadership would feel diminished for needing help. Retirement wasn't the end; it was a divine transition. I had spent years feeding others, developing leaders, and building infrastructure. Now, God was calling me to a new kind of service. There would be no annual reviews, no HR manuals, just me, God, and the people I was called to impact.

And then, as only God can, He confirmed it. On the very day of my retirement, my phone rang. It was the Richland Library, asking if I would interview for a temporary Entrepreneur-in-Residence position, a role designed to pour into local entrepreneurs: to guide, to coach, to equip.

I said yes. God was at work. He opened a door I never saw coming and did it on the very day I stepped out in faith. I've come to believe something deep in my soul: when you say yes to God's timing, you won't miss what He has in store. The position was rich in impact. I met men and women with dreams they had never spoken aloud. I helped them clarify their company visions and mentored people who were exactly where I had once been scared, uncertain, and full of potential.

Through it all, I remember that this is still not mine, it's God's. The work continues. The assignment evolves. The truth remains: God honors obedience.

He moves when you move with Him. He blesses what you place in His hands.

Starting my business was an act of faith.
Retiring was an act of surrender.
And walking into this new season?

That was an act of trust.
The journey isn't over, because when God writes your story, every ending is just the beginning of something greater.

The Power You Carry

There's a truth I didn't always have words for I could only feel it.

It was in the hallway when no one came back for me.

It was in the silence when someone finally did.

It was in the candy bar, a small reminder that I mattered.

I've shared some heartbreaking and heart-healing moments that shaped who I am today. Over time, I've come to understand that every moment, whether we're aware of it or not, is forming something profound. My life reflects the *Power of Living Your Purpose* and is a blueprint for what I call PRESENCE.

This isn't just a concept. It's a lived framework, born from survival, shaped in leadership, and refined through years of walking with others through pain, transition, and calling.

PRESENCE is how we show up.

Not with answers, but with awareness.

Not with perfection, but with presence.

Whether you're a teacher in a classroom, a leader in a boardroom, a parent, a social worker, or simply a human trying to hold it all together, your presence is never neutral. It either heals, harms, or helps. And once you see that, you can never unsee it. I didn't write this book because I thought I had it all figured out. I wrote it because I lived it. Because I'm still living it. And because I believe:

We don't need more people who know what to do.

We need more people who know how to be.

To be still.

To be aware.

To be available.

To be safe.

To be present.

That's what PRESENCE invites us into:

Purpose awareness – Knowing why you're here, even when the "how" is unclear.

Resilience building – Learning how to bend without breaking.

Emotional intelligence – Sitting with others' pain without sinking into it.

Self-leadership – Being accountable for the energy you bring.

Empathy-driven communication – Speaking into silence with kindness and clarity.

Nervous system regulation – Returning to your body when the moment overwhelms you.

Consistency in character – Showing up even when it's hard.

Emergence and evolution – The continual unveiling and refining of your authentic self.

These are the threads that run through every chapter you just read. Now, they are tools you can carry forward.

If my story moved you, I am grateful. More than that, I hope it stirred something within you, a longing to show up differently, more intentionally, not just for others, but for yourself.

If you're ready to put presence into practice, the PRESENCE Framework workbook is available for you. It's filled with exercises, tools, and space to wrestle and reflect. Whether you're working through it alone, using it in your organization, or leading a team, it serves as a companion for your work and life journey.

If you're a leader, formally or informally, who wants to bring this kind of transformation to your school, workplace, or community, I would love to walk with you.

You don't need the perfect words. You don't need to fix everything. You need to be present, and that alone can make a profound difference.

Thank you for walking with me as I shared the power of living in my purpose.

Now, walk with someone else.

Your presence is more powerful than you think.

To learn more about the PRESENCE Framework, workshops, or to book Donna Davis for your next conference or event, contact her at dwdavisconsults@gmail.com and follow her on LinkedIn: https://www.linkedin.com/in/donnadavispresents/

Epilogue: She Still Matters

You may not be able to go back and change the past, but you can go back and love the child who lived through it.

I see her now, clearer than ever.

The girl with the brave eyes and tired spirit. The one who showed up for life when life didn't show up for her. The one who smiled on cue, spoke softly so she wouldn't seem like too much, stayed quiet when the world told her she wasn't enough.

She didn't know what she was surviving at the time. She only knew how to keep going.

She didn't know that one day she'd lead rooms, not just sit in the back of them. That she'd write books, not just underline someone else's. That she'd no longer wait for an invitation, because she was the invitation.

She didn't know that God was saving every tear, every sigh, every half-whispered prayer into her pillow. That every night she cried herself to sleep was being folded into a chapter of something sacred. That the candy bar she bought at the gas station wasn't just a treat, it was a testimony, a holy act of survival, a whispered rebellion against despair.

She didn't know that the very things meant to destroy her would one day become the same things God would use to deliver others. She didn't know.

I know what it's like to feel forgotten, to walk through life as if healing is for everyone else. To wonder if the weight you carry is just too heavy to be free.

I also know what it's like to be met suddenly and softly by the God who remembers who reaches back through the years and gathers the broken pieces, who kneels beside the child inside of you and says, "I never left you."
And that's why I'm here. That's why I wrote this book. Not to show you how far I've come, but to remind you how deeply, how abundantly, you are loved.

You don't have to pretend anymore.
You don't have to power through.
You don't have to be the strong one all the time.

It's okay to sit with your younger self and cry the tears you never felt safe to cry.

It's okay to grieve what you never received.

It's okay to name what hurts and allow yourself to heal.

And just in case no one ever told you:

You were brave to survive.

You are wise to heal.

You are enough to begin again.

If you take nothing else from these pages, take this:

God wastes nothing.

Not your pain.

Not your past.

Not even the pauses when it felt like nothing was happening at all.

He has been writing beauty into your story all along. Even now, He is not done.

So, breathe. Let the tears fall. Let the walls come down.

And when you're ready, reach back for your younger self. Whisper these words:

"You made it. I see you now. And I promise I will never leave you behind again."

This is your moment not to finish, but to begin again.

A Final Word from Donna

If you're holding this book, I invite you to pause and take a breath. You've made it through every chapter, every valley, every "Get Up" moment. You've endured things you don't feel safe talking about, and you've carried hope even when your hands were full of disappointment.

You're still here. I wrote these pages not just to reflect, but to reach the part of you that might still be wondering if you're worthy of more. You are.

God has not forgotten you. You are not too late.
With love and unwavering belief in you,
Donna

Special Acknowledgment

In memory of my parents, Daniel White and Betty Lee White There aren't enough pages in this book to hold what you poured into my life.

Thank you for loving me in ways that didn't always come with big words, but shone through enormous sacrifices, long nights, and gentle reminders that I mattered. You gave me a childhood rich in faith, kindness, and dignity, even when money was tight and life was heavy. I always felt covered.

Mom, thank you for being the heart of our home, for turning Sunday mornings and Vacation Bible School into sacred spaces of joy and nourishment. I learned ministry by watching you serve. Thank you for letting me know you were watching my broadcasts every time I went live, commenting, "Mom is watching." Oh, how I miss talking to you and spending Thanksgiving with you.
Dad, thank you for checking my bookbag as if it were your job, and for reminding me, without fail, that I could become anything I set my mind to. Thank you for those candy runs on payday that

made ordinary days feel magical. I miss our Saturday morning calls and remember our last one. You said it was a beautiful day, and we didn't know it would be your last.

You both gave me a foundation to stand on. Everything I've become carries your imprint. Every room I walk into, I carry your love with me. This story may have my name on the cover, but it was written with the legacy of your love. I know I am well-loved.

Donna

www.ingramcontent.com/pod-product-compliance
Lightning Source LLC
Chambersburg PA
CBHW060047230426
43661CB00004B/695